D0882787

THE IMAGINATION ON TRIAL

The Imagination on Trial is a series of discussions with twelve contemporary British and American writers, which by exploring individual working methods aims to show how a writer's ideas germinate and develop. Each of the writers included has taken fiction into new and exciting territory: J.G. Ballard, Alan Burns, Eva Figes, John Gardner, John Hawkes, Wilson Harris, B.S. Johnson, Tom Mallin, Michael Moorcock, Grace Paley, Ishmael Reed, Alan Sillitoe.

As a novelist himself, Alan Burns discussed the problems confronting contemporary writers with a number of practising novelists in England, and after moving to the United States in 1977 to take up a teaching post at the University of Minnesota, he joined forces with Charles Sugnet, a colleague in the English Department, to widen the scope of the conversations to include some of North America's leading writers. Together they edited several years' accumulation of unique material (sadly, two of the novelists interviewed died before this volume could be published); Charles Sugnet contributes a stimulating Introduction that sets the writers in the context of post-war fiction and introduces them to British and American readers and the book is completed by a discussion in which Alan Burns answers many of the questions he has put to other writers.

The result is a fascinating book which sheds light on the creative process in general and in particular on the difficulties and rewards of being an imaginative writer today.

THE IMAGINATION ON TRIAL

British and American writers
discuss their working methods

ALAN BURNS and CHARLES SUGNET

Allison and Busby
London & New York

First published 1981 by
Allison and Busby Limited
6a Noel Street, London W1V 3RB, England
and distributed in the USA by
Schocken Books Inc.,
200 Madison Avenue, New York, N.Y. 10016

British Library Cataloguing in Publication Data
    The imagination on trial.
    1. English fiction — 20th century — History and criticism
    2. Authors, English — 20th century — Interviews
    3. Authors, American — 20th century — Interviews
    I. Title
    823'.9'1209   PR884   80-49689

    ISBN 0-85031-383-X
    ISBN 0-85031-384-8 Pbk

Printed in Great Britain by
Biddles Ltd, Guildford and King's Lynn

Contents

The authors wish to acknowledge the generous co-operation of the writers who are the subject of this book: J.G. Ballard, Eva Figes, John Gardner, Wilson Harris, John Hawkes, B.S. Johnson, Tom Mallin, Michael Moorcock, Grace Paley, Ishmael Reed, Alan Sillitoe. Wilson Harris invented our title during his conversation with Alan Burns.

We gratefully acknowledge financial and other assistance received from The Arts Council of Great Britain, The Phoenix Trust (Society of Authors) of Great Britain, the McMillan Fund, University of Minnesota, U.S.A., and the English Department of the University of Minnesota.

Our thanks to John Edgar Tidwell and Tom Meersman of Minnesota Public Radio, and to Steve Benson of radio station KUOM.

Preface

The Imagination on Trial does not set out to be a critical work. It tries to show how a fiction writer's ideas germinate and evolve. B.S. Johnson describes how for him the process starts, the moment of recognition: "Ah! That's the start of a novel. Ah! There's an image I can use." It was *that moment* that interested me most in talking with these writers.

My original intention was to focus on British novelists only, but I had the opportunity to widen the scope of the book when I moved to the University of Minnesota in 1977. There I met Charles Sugnet, a colleague at the English department, and he helped select and contact the American writers, and together we edited the raw material. The talks on which the book is based range over several years, from 1973 onwards. The time span and the book's transatlantic character have, I hope, made fashion, than would otherwise have been possible. The reader can compare the working methods of Englishman Alan Sillitoe with the American John Gardner; Eva Figes talks in the early seventies, Grace Paley in 1979.

My friendship with many of the British writers and sad recollection of the early death of two of them make it hard for me now to see this group in perspective. Charles Sugnet does that job in the Introduction that follows.

A.B. 1981

Introduction

Tony Tanner has written in the *New York Times* Book Review about the incongruity of reading William Burroughs's *Naked Lunch* while looking out over the pastoral grounds of King's College, Cambridge, which still maintains a small flock of actual sheep to complement the enormous number of its clerical pastors. However out of place Burroughs may seem in such an artificial paradise, he found a place in the rest of Britain: he is the writer most frequently mentioned by the British novelists interviewed in this volume. Tanner himself found Burroughs's obscene surrealism more energetic and closer to the realities of his own life than the placid lawns. The incongruity of Burroughs's writing may be obvious from Oxbridge or an English country house. But if you live under London's Hammersmith flyover, or below water level amid the reservoirs of Shepperton and Staines, Burroughs fits right into your native landscape. As these interviews demonstrate, many contemporary British writers are responding to the surreality of urban existence under late capitalism.

Yet the prevailing image of England among Americans, even those who have struggled from Heathrow to Earl's Court via Hammersmith, is still close to the pastoral of King's College, a combination of high culture with the "green and pleasant land", which even in Blake's day was disappearing. The prevailing American myth about British fiction is that it remains traditional, nostalgic, even stodgy. If you are an American undergraduate interested in "serious" or "experimental" fiction, your instructors will direct you to French works by Robbe-Grillet, Sarraute, Beckett, Butor, and younger writers like Monique Wittig or Philippe Sollers.They will assume your familiarity with certain North Americans (Pynchon, Hawkes, Barth, Coover) and will recommend the Latin Americans: Borges, Fuentes, Cortazar and especially Garcia Marquez. Will they recommend any British writers? Perhaps Burgess, and maybe John Fowles who, by a wonderful sleight-of-hand, writes stories that satisfy traditional readers while at the same time conspicuously reminding the others that he *has* read Heisenberg and Barthes.

As for the rest of the British, such a student might be told, read them if you like country-house novels; if you enjoy a solid though outdated social reality; if you like satire based on firmly held standards; if you like moral introspection that is conscious, explicit, and highly serious; if you like writers who pretend that *Ulysses* had never been written. This history, as Blake says about the Bible, has been adopted by both parties. I have some acquaintances who deliberately avoid contemporary French and American novels, preferring the British because of their supposed conservatism. Such readers devour Graham Greene, Kingsley Amis, Margaret Drabble, and even C.P. Snow, because those writers construct what such readers call "reality", meaning the world they try to persuade themselves they live in. The more sophisticated of them admit that certain forms are genre escapism, like the detective story. Others, Anglophile professors, insist that the life described in such books is "reality". They have apparently reduced their own American, urban, bureaucratized lives to the status of shadows on the wall of the cave. As Alan Burns says in his discussion with J.G. Ballard, "for many readers, the anachronistic character of the nineteenth-century novel is the basis of its appeal." My acquaintances would add that England is the country where the nineteenth century remains unchallenged.

There are several reasons for this continuing (and inaccurate) American belief about British fiction. Some of it is due to reactionary nostalgia for a caste system, particularly among professors and intellectuals who want to see themselves as the last leisured class, an aristocracy of taste. There is plenty of understandable nostalgia for the good, simple, old certainties, which may not have been either simple or good but can look so in retrospect. Moreover, it is a cliché of American fiction studies, taken from Hawthorne's preface to *The House of the Seven Gables*, and expanded by several academic critics, that Americans write "romances" (flights of New World fancy taken in the absence of a social structure), while Englishmen write "novels" (realistic studies of grown-up manners and morals in a stable social situation) because they have the class system America lacks. A believer in these categories would find it unsettling to discover Englishmen writing like Burroughs. There are also the economics of publication and distribution, which ensure that Americans simply never hear of many good British writers.

So it came as a surprise to this American reader to discover, through the accidents of talking with Alan Burns, reading Giles Gordon's collection *Beyond the Words* and meeting Ian McEwan, that there is already a substantial body of good recent British fiction which corresponds roughly to the American work discussed in Tony Tanner's *City of Words* — work which in the U.S. would be called "experimental" or "postmodern" or some such jargon. The degree to which these writers remain unknown even to well-informed American readers can be measured by the fact that the library at my absurdly large university, a library which "boasts" (as the phrase goes) over four million volumes, does not list a single title by B.S. Johnson in its catalogue. Yet the language and concerns of these novelists would strongly interest the same readership which buys Hawkes, Pynchon, Coover and Gaddis. They too offer an investigation of the country we all live in, the country of freeways and billboards, of racism and pop culture, of labour disputes and military atrocities, a country where mass-produced language pours out of radio and television, piling up like uncollected garbage.

The variety, deliberateness and intelligence of this investigation on both sides of the Atlantic is evidenced by these interviews. Local differences are important. They will continue to exist in spite of the homogenizing tendencies of mass culture, and they will be essential to our survival. But the novel has become inter-national. This is not merely because writers read each other, so that Beckett influenced B.S. Johnson, or Faulkner affects Garcia Marquez. Nor is it a matter of specific similarities (Hawkes and Ballard both fascinated with auto wrecks, Pynchon and Ballard both using clinical language to describe human bodies) or even of a common repertoire of shared images and subjects (Marilyn Monroe, the Kennedys, etc.). It is, rather, a matter of the way the common pressures of history result in certain shared attitudes. Central to these attitudes lately is the assumption that "reality" is not a fixed starting point from which mimesis can proceed, but is instead an open question itself. When Wilson Harris says the imagination is on trial, he isn't using "imagination" in the old romantic sense of a special creative faculty possessed by a few sensitive individuals. He isn't just talking about the continued production of that special class of objects we call "art". He is discussing the way in which the whole public has been conned (or has conned itself) into accepting as fixed, "natural", and "real", an order of things which is a human artefact. Eva Figes, when asked to pinpoint the insight which made it possible for her to write, describes the moment when she saw through this deception: "I discovered that life was not con-tinuous, that the novels of the past were portraying a false reality."

"People take so many things for granted," Harris says. "If you walk down a street, you take the trees for granted, but . . .in a strange way you are quoted into the street. Because people have been living in this place for centuries . . . in fact, there's a subjectivity written into it by men, generation after generation, century after century, yet people *accept*. They accept institutions

like they accept a hill." Obviously, when the institutions being
accepted are the Pentagon, apartheid, or sexism, such acceptance
is dangerous. One of the social artifices too often accepted as a
"natural" fact through failure of imagination is the second-class
status of women. A writer like Grace Paley, who debunks the
masculine, heroic, kind of literature, and who lets women speak
in their own voices, is helping us to reimagine the world, to
refuse passive acceptance. In the discussion reprinted here,
Paley, a determined resister of war and other insane masculine
inventions, shows how this reimagining of the domestic places
domestic life at the centre of politics and history.

For Harris, and to some extent for Ishmael Reed, freeing us
from such blind acceptance involves a kind of archaeology, a
research into the historical past to expose and reorder the images
we take for granted. Harris describes a beautiful instance of this
process, relating how he saw a fire-eater in the streets of
contemporary Mexico City, how the fire the man eats is related
to the sun-worshipping Aztecs who founded the city, and how the
Aztecs are in turn related to the government's fine arts building,
which is slowly sinking back into the mud of the Aztec lake under
the contemporary city. When Harris has finished, it is no longer
possible to take Mexico City for granted. Starting from a street
scene any tourist might think as solid as the city's buildings, he
unravels the subjectivity which has been written into that scene
until finally the buildings themselves begin to float in the
imagination. It's easier to take things for granted in your home-
land, and this may be one reason why exile has been an advantage to many twentieth-century writers.

J.G. Ballard, himself a permanent exile from the China of his
childhood, refers in a different way to the subjectivity written
into our surroundings when he says: "The writer's job is no
longer to put the fiction in. . . . People have enough fiction in
their lives already, they're living the stuff, it's pouring out of the
air, it's affecting everything, the ways people furnish their homes,
the sorts of friendships they have, their vocabularies. It's quite
amazing to see how people's lives are influenced by movies, television and constant advertising." Of course, the various means of
reproduction and transmission invented in the last two hundred
years have made more fictions available to us; some of the consequences of this development were described by Walter Benjamin
in his essay on "The Work of Art in the Age of Mechanical
Reproduction". Industrialization has affected more than the
transmission of fictions: their very production has been industri-
ally speeded up and transformed by modern advertising and

public relations. As John Hawkes says, "We are living imagined lives which we imagine".

Ballard discusses this new kind of fiction-making, using the example of the airlines and the detergent industry: "You don't buy an airline ticket just to take you from London to New York any more — what you're buying is an image of a certain kind of transportation style. The food, the in-flight movies, the steward-esses' uniforms, all contribute to a fiction designed to serve an imaginative aim. . . . (People) don't want Square-Deal Surf, as Lever Brothers found to their cost. Housewives don't want a square deal, they want glamour and excitement, and Daz and Omo give them that."

Ballard recommends "investigative, analytic techniques" to examine these fictions and make readers aware of the subliminal furniture they are taking for immutable reality. An early Ballard story, "The Subliminal Man", concerns a society in which every-one is working himself crazy to pay for consumer goods that people buy like zombies because of powerful subliminal messages beamed from huge billboards along the freeways. Accepting the subliminal message is mistaking someone else's fiction for "reality", and "taking things for granted". The analytic alterna-tive is suggested by Ballard's *Atrocity Exhibition*, which contin-ually manipulates certain images (Brigitte Bardot's body, Ronald Reagan's face, Jackie Kennedy in her bloodstained clothes, Vietnamese war victims, auto crashes) in an investigation of the violent psychosexual foundation of media politics and pop cul-ture. The investigation also returns to the mad consumerism which concerned him in "The Subliminal Man", and reveals the fetishism of consumer behaviour. (At one point, a character speculates on the future of sex with objects: "It's an interesting question — in what way is intercourse per vagina more stimu-lating than with this ashtray, say, or with the angle between two walls?") By holding up such images for examination in the deliberate art of his atrocity exhibition, Ballard acknowledges their importance, but also demonstrates that they are not necessary or inevitable. They are, instead, a series of billboards which can be modified or taken down and replaced if we refuse their subliminal messages. After reading Ballard, it is hard to take consumer products or the highway system for granted.

A modern "atrocity exhibition" based on popular imagery is bound to contain "second-hand things". Such "second-hand things" have been a part of literature at least since Flaubert described Emma Bovary's second-hand objects of desire. Second-hand bits, however primly footnoted, make up Eliot's wasteland.

Joyce, in *Ulysses*, threw away the quotation marks and simply incorporated things (headlines, adverts, soft-core pornography, etc.) into his book without attributing any ownership beyond that which we all have in common. Since then, the industrial acceleration in the creation of fictions has nearly drowned us in second-hand words and images; the word "cliché" is itself derived from an industrial noise made in the process of casting stereotype printing plates. One reason for Burroughs's success is that he has made such verbal borrowings into weapons in his guerrilla war against mass communications. He used to travel with trunks full of texts from what he called "the Senders"; these were cut up in small bits and folded back into his own work. He has used tape-recorders to splice pieces of text, with the same point: to use cliché against cliché, to use the machine against the machine, to send the second-hand messages back transformed.

The exhibition of "second-hand things" can easily lead to psychological analysis of a whole culture. One of the complaints made about Freud (with only partial justice) is that he was too interested in discovering pathology's origin in the particular stories of middle-class individuals. Joyce's nighttown, Genet's *Balcony* and Burroughs's *Naked Lunch* offer that "pathology" as norm rather than aberration, and find its origin in the shape of the whole culture, rather than in something exclusively personal. Poldy Bloom as Mayor of Dublin and Poldy Bloom as degraded execution victim map not only the fantasy limits of Poldy's psyche, but also the actual structure of the Irish polity.

Nearly all the writers interviewed here show a strong sense of the importance of unconscious and irrational forces. Some, like Sillitoe, tiptoe carefully around those forces, accepting their power but preferring to let them operate without the writer's conscious awareness. Others approach the unconscious deliberately, armed with snatches of Freud and a surrealist willingness to trust themselves to chance. None of these writers seem to have any neat explanatory theory of the unconscious, or any illusions about carrying the strong light of a modern electric torch to the back of the cave. The clinical simplifications about sickness and health seem to have disappeared. Several writers find value in forms of erotic behaviour conventionally thought of as perverse. Hawkes calls the strange William Hencher "the true lover" in *The Lime Twig*, and has elsewhere indicated that voyeurism is an acceptable expression of love; Ballard tries to find a use even for the vicarious sadomasochism of televised war atrocities.

Rather than imposing over-neat theories, the essential thing is to trace the lines of force which connect the private nighttown to public behaviour. For Ishmael Reed, this may mean building a contemporary narrative around an explanatory African myth, or rewriting the pious movie versions of American history to show sexual and economic truths of racism. For Ballard, it necessitates the use of newspaper clips, political clichés, and other fragments to show how erotic energy is mobilized for war, for industrial production, and for consumerism. Perhaps "tracing the lines of force" implies more continuity than is appropriate to this process. The phrase "velocity of a dream" comes up in several interviews, suggesting not only speed, but also the discontinuity, the uncontrollability, the enigma of dream. The fictional process of making these connections is also discontinuous, like guerrilla warfare, with an explosion here, an illumination there. Suddenly, by an inspired juxtaposition, the car crash becomes an orgasm, the panty-hose commercial turns into de Sade, Uncle Sam's pointing finger is revealed as the penis-gun it so obviously always was, and the images cannot be taken for granted again.

Subliminal messages are dangerous, then, but they can be neutralized by the use of what Ballard calls "analytic techniques". Burroughs has systematized his (and our) paranoia about such messages in his myth of the Senders and the Receivers in *Naked Lunch:* the way to fight the Senders (Hawkes calls them "mimes") is to cut up their message and send it back in altered form. The "cut-up" or "fold-in" techniques Burroughs developed literally involve making a collage out of bits of your own text interspersed with shards of other texts — pieces from newspapers and Joseph Conrad novels. By cutting your own text too, you work against the tendency of any writer to become a tyrannical Sender. The problems of power are in the language itself, and Burroughs believes you must cut the phrases up, submit even your own writing to some element of chance. Orwell recognized the problem when he talked in "Politics and the English Language" of phrases that lie around like so many gummed labels waiting to be pasted together. Good writers are always fighting this tendency; when Beckett, for instance, refers to a character's birthplace as the town where he first saw "the murk of day", Beckett is fighting the optimistic assumptions built into the cliché. But the difficulty and the political urgency of this task increase as the twentieth century continues.

Most of the writers interviewed here would agree that the problematic reality people take for granted is often textual in form. Note, for instance, the verbs used by Wilson Harris: "you are *quoted* into the street . . . there's a subjectivity *written* into it by men . . . ." However, there is considerable hesitation about adopting Burroughs's method; a good political and artistic argument can be made for simplicity and accessibility to a broad group of readers. Alan Sillitoe insists on the need for a classical clarity in treating his unclassical subject matter: "I have this prejudice, call it what you will: what you read in print must be fairly easily understood . . . . I want to maintain whatever clarity I can produce." Communication, accessibility, and rapport with readers are obviously important to Michael Moorcock, too, though his stylistic surfaces may be more varied than Sillitoe's. While Ballard is willing to cut up and redeploy pop images, to use and parody the language of science, he makes it explicit that he is not willing to pursue his experiments to the sentence level.

B.S. Johnson *is* willing to experiment with fractured sentences, and he's brilliantly successful at it, but these experiments are, I believe, based on traditional notions of artistic control and expressiveness. In the jargon of the American academy, Johnson would probably be called "modernist" rather than "post-modernist". He's read Beckett carefully, and the effects show in his work. But Beckett, in his dialogues with Georges Duthuit, insisted on the writer's inability to express, whereas it seems to me Johnson's experiments are done in the name of expressiveness and are usually mimetic. His characteristic ellipses, for example, are usually used to indicate the pauses, blanks, and transitions in the flow of consciousness. Even in the extreme of *House Mother Normal*, where he's attempting to reproduce the state of not-quite-consciousness of senile inhabitants of a nursing home, the series of dots which sometimes go on for pages may still be said to *represent* or *express* the blankness and temporary emptiness of those fading minds. Johnson is a superb reinventor of form, either at the sentence level or at the level of overall organization (as in *The Unfortunates*, his excellent unbound novel-in-a-box). But he reinvents form in the classical modernist way, in relation to content, in order to express content. Eva Figes has a similar aesthetic, trying to exercise rigorous control over even the sounds of syllables, so that her writing can, like music, express pure emotion.

If certain verbal formulations constitute both a cultural prison *and* the writer's means of "communication", what shall he or she do? Even relatively successful and accessible writers seem to feel left out of the mainstream and disconnected from their potential audience (though this may be less true of women writers, since feminism has created an audience for them). B.S. Johnson says he writes for himself, to work things through, implying that such a private exercise would have value even if the work were not read: but it's hard to believe the B.S. Johnson who wrote passionately about class warfare, and insisted he would never desert his side in it, could be content to write only for himself. Sillitoe, Ballard, and others express uneasiness about reviews, sales and readership. Some of this is the normal shoptalk of people who make their living by writing, but I think there's more to it than money or even fame. This worry about disconnection from an audience is rooted in questions about the status of the novel itself. Ballard astutely observes that the "sales" of high-art novels wouldn't be much better if they were given away. The problem is not money, he says, but people's interest: "the decline of the mainstream novel [is] not just in terms of its sales, but the role it plays in people's imaginations." One evidence of this is that so many of these novelists incorporate things from the movies, popular literature, television and advertising. Fifty years ago, the movies borrowed from the novel; now, it often works the other way around. (Tom Mallin imitates the form of the screenplay in his novel *Dodecahedron*.) This is one of the many indications that the novel no longer retains its cultural centrality, no longer articulates the fantasy structures which shape our lives. This function has been taken over by the movies and the mass media. As Ballard puts it: "I sensed way back in the late fifties, when I started, that the tide was running away from the written word towards the visual mode of expression." To an increasing degree, the novel analyses and investigates structures of meaning articulated elsewhere.

There is a good deal of unease among these writers about their place and status, about whether they are reaching the proper public, or indeed, whether they are reaching any public at all. This is why both Ballard and Moorcock recall with fondness writing for science-fiction magazines, where there is a real, steady audience. Moorcock knows the members of that audience; he can predict their tastes, and can describe ways in which he tried to modify those tastes. Ballard remarks with fascination that it would be possible, by looking at the magazine's subscription files, to learn exactly who your individual readers are.

The magazine format connects the anxious writer with an observable public, and science fiction has continued to be a "popular" genre with a consistent following. There are many reasons for this. Almost from its beginnings, SF has expressed our culture's unacknowledged guilt at the Faustian tamperings of science. It has become what Michel Butor, in *The Crisis in the Growth of Science Fiction*, calls "the normal form of mythology in our time", and it has been a useful vehicle for certain types of erotic fantasy. Sometimes, as in Ballard's "The Subliminal Man",

SF is used as a serious tool to project or extrapolate the future from our current situation. A writer like Burroughs can use the imagery of grade-B science fiction to express the horror of our total need — we ectoplasmic junkies of late capitalism, addicted to chemicals, consumer goods, mass-produced words, power: Western culture as the green blob that swallowed New Haven! At its worst, science fiction is as predictable as other pop genres, and a reader can take much for granted, but at its best it provides, in addition to all its other uses, a set of metaphors for alienation, and a perfect technique for expressing alienation. What is it like to live on a planet where all planning starts from the imperatives of the machine? What is it like to live in a world where your evolved biological responses are irrelevant? How does it feel to be utterly different from the other creatures around you? Science fiction was invented to explore such questions. Whether you define alienation biologically, personally, economically, or metaphysically, science fiction is well equipped to express it.

In this way, SF parallels the great project of the "serious" avant-garde, which was founded on its deliberate (but ambivalent) separation from bourgeois society. Certain recent texts by Beckett are both serious avant-garde writing *and* a kind of science fiction creation of the alien universe. *The Lost Ones* and *Imagination Dead Imagine* both describe strange planets which are in some way our own planet with nothing taken for granted. Beckett's more recently published "fizzle 1", in which a consciousness with an apparently human body feels its way down a ditch or tunnel, has all the rigour of a stark science fiction. Perhaps "science fiction" is what happens any time a writer stops taking the known world for granted and begins to explore. In Borges's story "Tlon, Uqbar, Orbis Tertius", science fiction is a metaphor for all fiction; and Butor, himself a serious novelist who has written on science fiction, suggests a similar convergence in an essay called "The Novel as Research".

There are a number of paradoxes in this relation between science fiction, alienation and "serious" fiction. The one most relevant to the remarks of the writers interviewed here is that for the SF writer there may be a community of alienation, an audience for alienation, like the one the avant-garde writer wishes he had but doesn't. John Gardner attempts to resolve this problem, not by becoming a science-fiction writer but by forsaking the traditional avant-garde stance toward bourgeois morality and returning to old verities. He is a professor of medieval literature as well as a novelist, so for him those old verities are not so much the social certainties of nineteenth-century realism as they are the moral certainties of an even earlier period. Fantasy literature is fine with Gardner, but he wants the fantasy to be moral and to offer the reader models for the conduct of his or her own life. In recent books (especially in *On Moral Fiction*), and in interviews, Gardner has elaborated this idea, has become controversial by attacking fellow novelists explicitly, and by condemning modern fiction as "tinny, commercial, and immoral". This does not, he says, "follow from a sickness of society, but the other way around . . . real art creates myths a society can live by instead of die by. . . . Moral fiction holds up models of decent behaviour."

Burns's discussion with John Gardner avoids most of this polemic and concentrates instead on Gardner's own work and working methods, which are interesting. The careful reader will still see signs of the attitudes which have made him controversial. For Gardner, words like "good" and "decent", or phrases like "the very best novel" seem self-explanatory, whereas for many other writers the meaning of such terms is itself the problem. Gardner is ahistorical, seeming to assume that human responses now are about the same as they've ever been, and that fundamental events like courtship, marriage, or the birth of a child are constants. He seems to value his own and others' work according to how he imagines a reader will respond to it in fifty years, rather than by how it meets a current need; he writes for posterity, and judges novels by how well they transcend contemporary conditions, rather than by how they respond to those conditions. He mentions writers like Homer and Tolstoy frequently, placing himself and other contemporary writers in a scheme of "moral" world classics.

It is easy to see how comforting these notions would be to a novelist, since they offer to restore to him or her a central place in the culture, a place which has been decisively lost. They offer something even more attractive than the nineteenth-century mimetic scheme in which social reality was a fixed object to be imitated by a writer who occupied a privileged still point. They offer the writer an image of himself or herself as acknowledged legislator, moral arbiter, and to a certain extent, perhaps even priest. But I don't think it will work. Movies and television now occupy a good portion of the territory that once belonged to the novel; many of us are less certain about what is "decent" than Gardner seems to be; and many novelists can no longer see themselves as occupying a privileged, fixed, observation point. Their own situation and motives have begun to appear problematic; they suspect that they themselves may sometimes be the evil Senders. John Gardner may disagree with them, may not share their doubts, but it's no use accusing them of bad faith or commercialism — they see the world as they see it, and will continue to write from their own felt situations. For most contemporary writers, it would be bad faith (immoral, even!) to write as though they were medieval moralists and to misrepresent themselves out of a sense of duty. There is a great deal of moral concern among the writers interviewed here, but very little moral certitude. They have long since strayed from the theological universe where that kind of dogmatism was possible. Most of them are astray, interestingly astray, practising the fallen and doubtful art of fiction without help from Aquinas or Augustine or any other Father. Some, like Ishmael Reed, may become cultural entrepreneurs in an attempt to create the kind of subculture in which their writing matters; others, like Grace Paley, may work quietly at what they know best for years until they find that a community of readers has come into being for them, partially through their own effort.

These are courses of action rather than dogmatic positions, and it's obvious from the talks in this book that most writers work intuitively. If they make sweeping generalizations about their work at all (and some do not), the generalizations are *ex post facto*. Largely because of Alan Burns's interests as a fellow writer, these conversations contain a great deal more information about the specific ways a writer's intuition expresses itself as a working method, than is usually found in interviews. Alan and the writers he talks with make practical observations of the sort that other writers, especially younger ones, will find more useful to them than all the literary criticism in the world. Among the questions thus discussed: Where do the writer's ideas come from? How do writers work? At the typewriter? Pacing the garden? Do they ever abandon a book? Why? How many drafts do they do? How long does it take? What's the hardest part of the process? At what stage do they show the work to someone else? How well do they sleep at night?

These are important questions. Knowing that Sillitoe finds revising miserable, that Grace Paley puts stories aside and returns to them after longish periods of time — such apparently circumstantial details tell us a great deal about these writers and the nature of their work. They also tell us much about the nature of writing itself, and about the great variety of possible approaches to it. There is no one way to produce good writing, but here are twelve intelligent writers from both sides of the Atlantic, talking about how *they* do it.

Charles Sugnet, 1981

J. G. Ballard

J.G. Ballard was born in Shanghai of English parents in 1930, and remained there until he was sixteen. After two and a half years' internment in a Japanese prison camp, he was repatriated to England, where he studied at Leys School, Cambridge, and read medicine at King's College, Cambridge. He was married in 1953 and has four children; his wife died in 1966. Except for a brief period after the war as a Royal Air Force pilot, Ballard has always made his living as a writer. He has contributed to the leading science-fiction magazines and has had many collections of short stories published in Britain and the United States, including *The Terminal Beach* (1964), *The Disaster Area* (1967), *The Overloaded Man* (1968) and *Vermilion Sands* (1971). He is the author of eight major novels, among them *The Wind from Nowhere* (1962), *The Drowned World* (1962), *The Atrocity Exhibition* (1970), *Crash!* (1973), *Concrete Island* (1974) *High Rise* (1975) and the recently published *Hello America!* (1981).

Ballard is known as a science-fiction writer, popular and always in print, easily available in paperback to that group of bright students who read intelligent science fiction — Asimov, Bradbury and others. His work does not run to space warfare, and the strange creatures running amok in his books are not Martians but *us*. He has a strong grasp of scientific terminology, probably partly deriving from his medical studies, and he understands the distancing effect of such language. Ballard's first collection of stories, *The Voices of Time* (1962), was concerned with time distortions, and some critics found this limiting. A look at the titles above will easily show that his overriding interest has changed to place, and to a particular kind of landscape, the landscape of disaster, the waste land. The wasteland may be a beach or a remote airfield, but in his recent work the chances are good that it will be urban or suburban: one whole novel is set in a triangle of waste ground at the intersection of two motorways. Other stories concern themselves with those bleak bits of land around cities which most of us deliberately fail to notice as we drive quickly by. Ballard is interested in place, he has said, because of the way outer space can be used as a metaphor for inner space. The interview that follows frequently becomes a discussion about places, especially Ballard's home in Shepperton (southwest of London, in the pattern for Heathrow Airport) and the Shanghai which was his home and is lost to him.

BALLARD: Take the novel out of the context of the university Modern Literature Department, push back those plywood partitions and actually see the writer in his professional role, having all the problems (quite apart from the problems of writing) of persuading the publisher to publish what he's done — writing in the context of whatever one's doing. In my case, writing in the context, for years, of science fiction: science-fiction magazines, English and American anthologies, hardback and paperback, mainly paperback. And the whole social situation of the writer and the problems of the audience as well. Also the decline of the mainstream novel, not just in terms of its sales, but the role it plays in people's imaginations.

BURNS: *Its social relevance?*

Yes, the main underpinning of English culture for the last couple of centuries has been English literature. It has provided not only the literal vocabulary but also the yardsticks by which one's whole intelligent reponse to life is made. This applies not only to literary people but to anybody who is merely literate. Now this underpinning has completely gone, it's no longer part of the furniture of anyone's mind — anyone under the age of forty.

It's only a small minority of people who happen to be enthusiasts for English literature who read, who expect themselves to have read the whole body of English fiction and poetry. That's a huge revolution that's taken place. It makes the task of doing something new that much more urgent, trying to get back into the game, as it were, from the sidelines.

In the case of most novels published today, if they were free, if the publishers gave them away, their "sales" would be no higher. I don't think any more would be taken out of the bookshops if they were literally given away.

A question I'd like to discuss with you is the influence on your work of the place in which you live. A recurrent phrase in your book The Atrocity Exhibition, *a phrase with a good strong rhythm, like many of your phrases, is "The reservoirs of Shepperton and Staines".*

I was struck by the fact, when I came here, that I was living in a sort of marine landscape, most unusual. There are these enormous reservoirs, the nearest is only four or five hundred yards away, the Queen Mary Reservoir, which is a gigantic reservoir about a mile in diameter. The whole area in fact is infested with reservoirs and settling beds and conduits and little private canals. When you fly from London airport, when you look down while the plane circles around, you will see what looks like a huge expanse of water, with the Thames of course here too. In fact, we're living — we don't realize it — we're living on little causeways. There are huge gravel lakes as well; for a hundred years they've been digging sand out, and some of these old pits are damn big, ten times the size of the Serpentine. We're living in these houses, these little quiet suburban streets, which are little causeways running between these reservoirs. Most of them are invisible because there are high embankments for obvious reasons; the Water Board doesn't want people peeing in them, throwing cigarette ends in and so on. So they're well screened off, but one is aware of a sort of invisible marine world, of living below the water line. It works on you imaginatively after a while. This landscape — I think it's the most modern landscape in England in a way, because most of it was built in the thirties. In fact, most of it was probably built in the sixties, as far as houses and shops are concerned. It's built to a kind of Los Angeles pattern. Very poor public transport. It's full of people with cars. Everyone round here has a car, many families have two cars. It's all supermarkets, and rather nice-looking wives, about thirty, with two kids and a brand new Cortina. . . . A lot of people round here work either at the film studios or at the commercial TV studios, making TV commercials. And people work at the British Aircraft Corporation factory at Weybridge across the river — it's like Los Angeles, where everybody's working for Douglas Aircraft — it's a very curious zone, and there is a sort of life style here. It's almost post-TV, they don't bother to watch TV anymore. They're too busy with their squash on Monday nights, learning to water-ski on Tuesday, judo on Wednesday, party on Thursday, wife-swapping on Friday. They have no time to watch TV.

I may be imposing on your work — but I get this combination of the safe, domestic small-scale, right next door to the menacing large-scale, like the reservoirs, like the airport, and all the motor-way stuff.

Sure, it's a landscape governed by the motorcar. The new motorway is, well, you can almost throw a stone to it, just across these houses.

You've lived here for years. What about those other places that arise in your books, frequently. Like Eniwetok Atoll, where they tested the H-bomb. Have you ever been there?

No, the nearest I've been is about four hundred miles away, in China, in Shanghai. I was interned by the Japanese, with my parents.

You were born in Shanghai — do you remember the city?

Of course, I was sixteen when I left. It's extremely vivid. More real than this place in a way.

What does it do to you, that foreign origin?

It gives you a divided mind, there's no doubt about that. Very curious, actually, to spend your childhood and early adolescence in one place, and then never be able to go back to it. Because you can't, in a way, mature all those vintages or whatever you like to call them, that have been laid down. Large parts of you are forever . . . well, in a sort of artificially young state. I mean, I can go back in England, say, to see my old digs in Notting Hill, and I can see them with the eye of a mature man, seeing the penniless student living in a little rabbit hutch, who has since got married, had children . . . so in a way you mature that particular thing. By going back, in a sense you close it off. But if you're brought up abroad — even if I could go back now, I wouldn't be able to do anything, things have changed so much. It gives you a divided self and a whole set of potent images in one's mind.

That are still in movement, not settled?

Absolutely. I know that in my own writing, landscape, I don't mean merely physical landscape, psychological landscapes are very important to me. In a way, I am writing my *Amerika* without ever going there. All these inventions of imaginary landscapes are attempts to recreate that . . . .

Or to place yourself? To find your place?

To place oneself, to find oneself, to give oneself a certain sense and a set of map references, so one knows where one is! I had a very curious sensation several years ago, when I'd already lived in this house for about eight years. I took my children to Greece for a couple of months, down the Peloponnese where you've got these endless beaches which are totally deserted, rather uncanny in a way, because you've got this paradisial landscape, you expect to see centaurs, all sorts of mythological beasts. Standing on this totally deserted beach, I suddenly realized I'd forgotten where I lived in England. I *forgot*, it wasn't just a passing thing, I actually for about fifteen seconds couldn't remember where I lived. I had to work it out backwards — Boulogne, Dover, Vauxhall Bridge Road, Hammersmith Flyover. . . . Oh, of course! Shepperton! And I had to do that. . . . Curious . . . [*sighs*].

On the one hand England is your home country, on the other hand you are almost exploring a foreign land, trying to place yourself in it?

Yes, I still regard England as a foreign country.

One thing that strikes me about your descriptions of landscape — and Kafka and others did it — is that they are hard, physical, mathematical, scientific, irrevocably there . . . yet clearly nowhere, *clearly in a land of the imagination. This is certainly an aspect of your style, isn't it?*

I don't know how far any of it's calculated, though. I don't think it is. I don't set out to define, in the sense that an architect would, providing the specifications for the building, the curtain-walling, the under-floor heating that will use so many amps of current . . . . I don't set out specifications in that sense. It's just a matter of my style, I think.

A cool style. Its scientific precision distinguishes your work from that of many contemporary English novelists. Another way in which your work seems different from the others is that they seem more warm-hearted.

I regard myself as a very emotional person in my ordinary life. And I regard myself as a very emotional writer. I write out of what I feel to be a sense of great urgency and commitment. I'm certainly not a political writer, but I feel a great sense of urgency. One doesn't want to be too grandiose about it, but the moral and psychological pressure is very strong. When people say to me, "You're very cold and clinical," I always find that strange; they may be confused. I use the language of an anatomist. It's rather like doing a post-mortem on a child who's been raped. The anatomist's post-mortem is no less exact, he itemizes things no less clearly, for the rage and outrage he feels.

I've been surprised in talking to you, actually. I expected you to be much cooler, more analytical and self-mocking, but there's a degree of passion in your talk that is surprising.

Is it? I'm sorry it doesn't come through in the work. The topics my fiction covers are those I as an individual feel concerned about. They're summed up by all the fiction I've written. I can't really summarize them, fifteen books in fifteen minutes. When I began as a science-fiction writer, I felt that science fiction wasn't making the most of its own possibilities. It had become fantasy; its two main preoccupations were outer space and the far future, whereas in its best days it had always been a literature of commitment. I wanted to write a science fiction about the present day. My one ambition — I don't really feel I've achieved it — was to write an adult, mature, sophisticated science fiction. It's more difficult than you think, actually. Damn difficult, for very complicated reasons. Something about the cautionary tale, or expository fiction, that lends itself, that locks on like a damned leech, to all the worst elements, techniques, and devices that fiction has to offer: the too-contrived short story, the over-plotted narrative, and oh, all those other things. To write an oblique and open fiction in the cautionary mode is damn near impossible. But

I began writing science fiction about the present day. My first novels were obsessed with time, their real subject matter I suppose is time, the finiteness of life. But by the mid-sixties, I think the assassination of Kennedy acted as a kind of catalyst. It seemed to me that by that point the fictional elements of reality had begun to overwhelm the so-called "realistic" ones.

I thought the balance between reality and fiction had tilted by the mid-sixties so we were living inside an enormous novel. As I've said elsewhere, the writer's job is no longer to put the fiction in, the fiction's already *there*; the writer's job is to put the reality in. Every writer worth his salt has got to use investigative, analytic techniques, like a geographer facing an unmapped jungle, or a chemist faced with an unidentified but potent material. People have enough fiction in their lives already, they're living the stuff, it's pouring out of the air, it's affecting everything, the ways people furnish their homes, the sorts of friendships they have, their vocabularies. It's quite amazing to see how people's lives are influenced by movies, television and constant advertising. Politics is a branch of advertising, the whole thing is a hothouse of fictions. So one's role as a writer has radically changed, and the techniques of the nineteenth-century novel just aren't appropriate.

They're only appropriate in terms of nostalgia?

If you were writing a historical novel, or a multi-generation family dynasty sort of fiction . . . .

What I meant was that for many readers the anachronistic character of the nineteenth-century novel is the basis of its appeal. They wish to remain in that time when God was good and Britain was great; they delight in fiction which feeds that illusion. You use the word "fiction" to denote the half-life we live today, but another word is alienation.

By fiction I mean anything invented to serve someone's imaginative ends, or aims. For example, you don't buy an airline ticket just to take you from London to New York any more — what you're buying is an image of a certain kind of transportation style. The food, the in-flight movies, the stewardesses' uniforms, all contribute to a fiction designed to serve an imaginative aim. It applies to almost everything, from the launderette to Harold Wilson. As for, alienation, I'm not sure about that. I don't know if people today are any more alienated than they were before.

You are describing a situation of alienation because the fictions are being imagined, cooked up, by someone else for the consumer, to satisfy artificially created needs. Its aim is not to meet real need but to make a profit or secure control. Our real selves become masked by these lies, and we are alienated from our real needs and desires.

That's hard to say. I like Indian food, but that's not an artificial need, it's a genuine thing, a taste, though it was artificially imposed on me. I like American cars, I like their mastodonic outlines, etc. The American car is a complete artefact, of course, a fictional structure, a piece of sculpture, but that doesn't make it any less real. The Mona Lisa's pretty real to me.

I'm using the word "real" more in the Freudian sense of genuine wishes, real gratification of underlying infantile desires.

What you're saying is, are we having foisted on us a completely unreal world? I'm not so sure. There are unreal elements, fictions that don't work, but most of them do work. I think most people need Chinese take-aways, glammed-up packaged holidays . . . they'd much rather that. They don't want a square deal, they don't want Square-Deal Surf, as Lever Brothers found to their cost. Housewives don't want a square deal, they want glamour and excitement and Daz and Omo give them that.

To what extent do you try to give readers what they want? Are you concerned about that?

I don't write from any grandiose programs. I'm aware that I write from various obsessions — the elements that make up my own skull. I just write what takes my fancy and grips my imagination at any given time. Being originally a science-fiction writer, there's a cautionary element in whatever I do. It's not necessarily a moral; there's nothing moral about shouting: "Careful, there's a car coming." In respect to all these things like pollution and over-population and so on, one is pointing out ambiguities in our attitudes toward these things.

In Atrocity Exhibition, *you get pretty close to raw politics, with Ronald Reagan and the rest. Was there an abrupt change in your work at that point?*

Fair enough, though I went on writing conventional science fiction while I was writing that stuff. Those stories that make up *Atrocity Exhibition* — it's not a novel, that book, but it's not just a collection of short stories either — took four or five years to write. A lot of time went by very quickly while I was writing those stories. Because there's an awful lot there. There's an awful lot of material, and that material came out of years of thinking, imagining, living, and so on. Very important events were contracted into literally three paragraphs. It was very exhausting. Then I wrote *Crash!* It's an extension of all the ideas and arguments *Atrocity Exhibition* advances.

You talk of Atrocity Exhibition *in a way that I recognize; it is, as it were,* the *book. That's rather a grand thing and it can be a pretty bleak thing. It's all there . . . and from now on you've got to earn a living.*

No, no, no, no, no. *Atrocity Exhibition* and *Crash!*, in which I equate the crash with sexuality, were both extreme hypotheses, extreme metaphors to describe an extreme situation. Then my mind turned in other directions. It just happened.

When I said your work "took a turn", you didn't really account for it, you said "it happened". Now you're using the same phrase to describe your next turn. Can you go beyond that? Or would you rather not think about it?

I do think about it. I'm conscious of the fact that in the mid-sixties something happened to me. On a personal level, my wife's death, which coincided with the Kennedy assassination and the changing landscape of the sixties . . . my own life, my three children were very young when I . . . when my wife died. In my own life this appalling crime as I thought it against this woman had taken place, and to some extent against myself. And there seemed to be a kinship, this meaningless act of gratuitous violence seemed to have some kinship with the Kennedy assassination. And people were becoming dehumanized and overcerebralized; emotional responses to everything were becoming so stylized that we were moving into a kind of mad Nazi world. I think I was trying to make sense of my wife's death by taking as a subject matter the world of the 1960s, particularly that around Kennedy's death, and trying to make sense of it, trying to find in a paradoxical way something good. Now I know that's a sort of nightmare logic, but that's what *Atrocity Exhibition* is, a book of nightmare formulas. . . . Desperate, desperate measures — I suppose the whole of *Atrocity Exhibition* and *Crash!* is summed up under that heading. A kit of desperate measures, desperate devices.

Atrocity Exhibition was also part of your effort at personal survival? Did the book succeed at that in any measure for you?

I think it did. Now *Crash!* was a much more exhausting and deranging book to write . . . such an extreme metaphor . . . the effort of maintaining the logic of 2 plus 2 equals 5 or minus 7, or 99, anything but 4. I sort of hated myself as I wrote the book because I felt I was dealing in things, deadly things, like a sort of arms salesman. Much of the book was morally highly objectionable, there's no doubt about that. One of the publisher's readers was either a psychiatrist or the wife of a psychiatrist, and she wrote the most damning and vituperative reader's report they'd ever received. It included the statement: "The author is beyond psychiatric help." That's a pretty terrible thing to say about someone, particularly if you've got scientific qualifications. But I was quite pleased by the report, because it represents, in a sense, total artistic success. The book had *worked* if somebody could respond like that to it. But doing that book was morally and emotionally exhausting. I felt far better for it afterwards, though, like being swallowed by a whale and then climbing, cutting your way out again.

Was she implying that it's a deranged or evil book? Did she suggest that it would harm people?

I think it probably is an evil book, yes, it may be a corrupting book. But not too corrupting. If you read it, you'll see what I'm driving at. I'm trying to look at the sort of logic that allows — I think the latest figures published by the World Health Organization on automobile fatalities show that probably 250,000 people are killed, and that's probably an underestimate. *Millions* are injured, and seriously too. What logic is at work that allows this to happen?

I think we're all perhaps innately perverse, capable of enormous cruelty and, paradoxically (this is difficult to put into words), our talent for the perverse, the violent, and the obscene, may be a good thing. We may have to go through this phase to reach something on the other side, it's a mistake to hold back and refuse to accept one's nature. We're making a marriage, you know . . . the equation, sex times technology equals the future. This uneasy and sinister marriage between ourselves and technology is going to change all our values. We're living in an abstracted world, where there aren't any values, where rather than fall back, one has to immerse onself, as Conrad said, immerse onself in the most destructive element, and *swim*. Anyway, those books are in the past. I'm drawing breath before perpetrating another atrocity [*pause*].

On the cover of the Panther edition of Atrocity Exhibition, *the book is summarized and sold as "a novel". Yet you refer to it in the plural, as though it is a collection of pieces.*

Well, I don't know. In the strict, conventional sense of the term, it's not a novel. It doesn't have that self-conscious continuity that we tend to expect from a novel, but at the same time it's much more than just a collection of stories. They're all very tightly locked together. The whole thing reflects back on itself internally in all kinds of different ways. Partly, it's a conventional narrative with all the unimportant pieces left out. In the conventional novel there's far too much machinery, narrative machinery, narrative translational machinery, you know: "He went out of the door and down the steps. As he crossed the square, he saw his best friend approaching." I simply cut all that out. The modern mind is used to cutting, we're trained to accept not just cutting, but the tradition of modern sculpture, where mass is defined not by ten tons of basalt carved in a huge block but by a couple of apparently unrelated armatures. Also if you break up the narrative, you can rotate, each episode can be inspected from a number of angles. You don't have to look at the thing from one elevation. And I can annex a huge amount of material into the narrative using this method, which is one proof that it works. The category of the novel should be sufficiently elastic to accommodate what I did in *Atrocity Exhibition*.

In the conventional novel, there are limits as to how much you can jump around: you've got to maintain the stretched skin of the narration or the whole damned thing begins to sound funny. With the fragmented technique, you can move about in time, you can move from realism to fantasy, and you can play on the fact that it is sometimes difficult to tell what is "real", what is being presented as a piece of realistic narration and what is being presented as, say, the interior fantasy of one of the characters. And this reflects a characteristic ambiguity of everyday life today, when something is presented as sheer fantasy — watching Nixon on TV is just the crudest example. Is your doctor really trying to cure you or is he a sinister psychopath who is actually trying to maim you? Are the police defenders of right, or are they naturally professional criminals? Science fiction is full of these reversed roles, and you can play on these ambiguities. That's what the technique is about actually. Because I feel it reflects on modern life. The proof of the pudding is this: I feel that from *The Atrocity Exhibition* you could reconstitute the late sixties almost *in toto*, and get it all right. I don't mean the superficial aspects, but the whole psychology, the landscapes, the sum total of living, dreaming, dying during that period. That's a grandiose claim, but I may as well make it, dammit, it's my book. I'm not knocking Kingsley Amis or Iris Murdoch or Margaret Drabble, in fact I haven't read anything by any of them, but I don't believe from the majority of mainstream fiction — tiny, little, drying up — you could reconstitute the character of England. They're terribly parochial; it would be London probably, or Highgate. You could not reconstitute the England of the 1960s from the work of novelists who are reputed to most represent —

Social reality?

Yes. In a way it's a test. From Shakespeare you could reconstitute not just the superficial characteristics of the age, but its essence. Everything that was going on then is in those plays. The same is true of a very stylized writer, or one whose subject matter is treated in a very stylized way: Kafka. I feel you could reconstitute real life in Cracow or wherever he was living —

Prague. Actually, there's the whole of the twentieth century in Kafka.

Right, it's *there*. And in Burroughs!

The particular aspect you get from Kafka, and Burroughs, and from your book too, is that events move with such speed through such a range of extreme contradictions that one is left unsure of the nature of reality. Out there is moving, I'm moving, you're moving, so one's constantly unsteady, unstable, unsure. In your book, you get the reader to appreciate that experience because you're putting him on the spot, a particularly shaky spot, all the time.

Needless to say, I'm constantly getting people who say: "*Atrocity Exhibition*, oh, couldn't understand it, couldn't read it, impossible to read." I don't think it's a very difficult book; it's written in a very easy and open style. It's not difficult, but unfamiliar. This is where the experimental writer (it's not a term I like, but there doesn't seem to be any other) has the cards stacked against him. People are so lazy or so rooted in established conventions in their reading that they won't make the effort.

It's also fear. They would prefer not to have this question of unreality presented to them. It is rather worrying.

Fear too. And the separated paragraph form puts people off. People are used to having narration in short chapters, with a heading. Discontinuity worries them.

Your overall construction is fragmented and new and energetic and profoundly realistic, but when I look closer, at the sentences themselves — there's no fragmentation there. Why not be consistent and carry it further and break up the sentence too?

I quite see your point. It probably sounds preposterous, but I don't see myself as a literary writer (that's neither compliment nor criticism) and I don't want to write fiction that is in any way about itself. There are plenty of examples, not merely in the novel, but in music and painting. I'm tremendously responsive to painting of every school from Lascaux onwards. There's hardly a painter in the whole of the Renaissance I don't find some merit in, and almost every painter since Manet plays a vital role in my life, with the exception of abstract expressionism because that is painting really about itself. I want to avoid in my writing any hint of that. There are too many other things to be getting on with.

You would say, "The hell with it, there are more important things to talk and write about than the novel"?

Right. Now, I know there are writers interested in that sort of thing, and I don't want to put it down, but I think they're missing the point. I appreciate the difference between Manet and all his precursors, the frankness with which the modern painter acknowledges the nature of his paint surface. He doesn't say: "This is a piece of drapery." He says: "This is a piece of drapery *and* a paint surface." Fair enough, but I don't think one should get to the point where one is playing a whole series of conceptual games, elaborating a series of conceptual relationships about the nature of the medium itself. In this case, paint or words are our servants. They are not the subject, we are the subject.

In the summary which prefaces Atrocity Exhibition, *you say: "The central character is a doctor suffering from a nervous breakdown. His dreams are haunted . . . ." Are you betraying your work by suggesting that this smashed up or fragmented view of reality is a sick view, just as conventional writers will adopt a device — make him mad, make him drunk, make him concussed, say it's all a dream?*

I take the point. It occurred to me that I was perhaps too close to my Travis character . . . the whole thing just sprang out of the first story, which was "You and Me and the Continuum", and which actually is printed towards the end. Once I'd written about two of them, I saw the great breakthrough for myself that this technique represented. I suddenly had a completely new terrain.

Why are some passages, like the one beginning "In the suburbs of hell . . ." on p. 16, set in italics? I caught no more than a change of tone, but it brings to mind a problem I've also come up against. If you're going to make these paragraphs like this, then it's difficult to make a paragraph within that paragraph, to make a conventional indentation. You're compelled to make the whole separated section read straight through, but the demands of the narrative may mean that you don't always want to do that.

That's right. In the context of that "suburbs of hell" passage, I wanted to suggest a sort of mythological stratum . . . it's rather like a film, watching a film, where the action is suddenly overlaid by another image, just briefly, and one's conscious of a different system of time, perhaps a more dream-like atmosphere, something that touches another level of the mind, or what have you. To imply that the psychic levels have changed.

The term used in the book is "planes of consciousness", often a bit tongue-in-cheek?

If you take the Nathan character, Dr Nathan, who pontificates away throughout the book, now when the book was published, some people attacked it as being terribly pretentious, probably because they were thinking of the Nathan figure. Now Nathan's ideas are pretty close to my own, all the things Nathan says, I to some extent believe them too . . . .

You're also taking the mickey out of them to some extent?

Yes, that's the point I'm making, that I'm poking fun at my own ideas. There's a note of irony in the way Nathan's got it all tied up, the vocabulary he uses. He is an example of the pornography of science, and the particular vocabulary he uses, and the total detachment as he describes these horrendous events, it's an armchair view of damnation. I don't want to say he's my Dr Benway, because Benway is Burroughs's most powerful character. Nathan is a minor character in this book.

Nathan is a man who doesn't feel. Is there any character who does? Are they all tainted this way?

Travis is a sympathetic figure. He is the man, myself I suppose, who is aware of the nightmare, who is repelled by what seem to be the new logics unfolding. He has to go through all of them to find out what's on the other side. Maybe some of these desperate measures will work. He's like Schopenhauer's knight, in a way, beyond hope, but still riding on. His response is emotional. He abhors violence, he's not in any way attracted to it, he's repelled, but he's trying to understand what's happening.

The headlines to each paragraph are also ironic?

Of course: "The See-Through Brain", "The Sixty-Minute Zoom", "A History of Nothing". They're all meant to be ironic; practically no one saw that. *The Atrocity Exhibition* got some of the worst reviews I've ever seen in this country. I didn't worry. I was disappointed. As all the stories had been previously published, I'd already had a lot of response. If you write for a magazine, you have a visible readership, you can go to the offices and look at the subscription lists and actually know the names of those who read your stuff. And magazine readers are much more vocal than novel readers. The novelist has an invisible readership, this is part of the problem of being a novelist. We're living in an age of direct communication where everybody's in contact with everybody else. But the novelist. . . . Anyway, yes, I was disappointed, but the response on the continent was terrific, they were really tuned in, they used my language: "Media Landscape" and "On the Spinal Battlefield". They're the only reviews I've ever kept. Now, the response in this country was absolutely nil. Why?

Was this because they had the war on the continent, more physically and immediately?

Yes. And the world of the sixties materialized there almost overnight. My books explained that. Here it's different, we've been an imaginative satellite of the United States for thirty, forty years. We're rooted in the past. People here are slightly blotto. Changes are taking place, but they don't want to look too closely at them. They want to go on with their strange mixture of Sotheby's and Betty Grable and royal weddings. Oddly enough, *Crash!* had a much better reception. Curious. I don't spend my time moaning about reviews — partly as a result of having come up as a science-fiction fiction writer where you don't get any reviews. But some of the reviews of *Atrocity Exhibition* were absurd, absolutely ridiculous. I think it was the *Sunday Times* had a very dismissive piece by Julian Symons referring to my "evident relish for the nasty". He's a crime writer who spent his time writing not just novels but he actually published a book which I've got upstairs somewhere, called *Crime*. Great fat book, with hundreds of photographs, an encyclopedia of crime with descriptions of every conceivable criminal act from rape to mass murder. It's quite well done because it's got all the gory details: how many little girls this cannibal killer of Cologne ate between 1927 and 1933. This is a man who says I've got an evident relish for the nasty! That's one of the paradoxes: everything becomes so conventionalized that you can write about "crime". Very genteel and refined people make a living writing about crime for fifty years. Polite society allows this, no one raises an eyebrow. Someone comes along with a slightly fresh or original approach: "Oh, my god. Relish for the nasty." It's absurd. But *Crash!* had a much better response. Some people actually got the point. The man in *New Scientist* began: "This is the first pornographic novel based on technology." He absolutely got the whole thing; he really got it.

When you use figures like the Kennedys, Marilyn Monroe or Ronald Reagan as mythical characters in your work, are you concerned they'll become dated?

First, I'm not too concerned about posterity because I don't think we can plan ahead for what the future will find interesting in us. Making writing so generalized that it has no local connections doesn't necessarily increase its survival potential. But in the case of *Atrocity Exhibition* the odd thing is that the figures I selected as public personalities, like the Kennedys, Reagan, Elizabeth Taylor, are still in the news. I would guess in fifty years people will still know who the Kennedys, Elizabeth Taylor and Marilyn Monroe were. If one could look at the greatest: Shakespeare's plays are thick with topical allusions. The same is true of *Ulysses* — it's packed with local references which Joyce must have known would be meaningless to anyone who didn't know Dublin as well as he did. But that didn't matter. These are just the armatures that hold up the whole structure.

In so far as you have a certain attitude to and are processing material that derives from the media, these sensational myth figures are bound to crop up, because the media personalizes news in that way . . . you say your language isn't "literary" and I accept that, but there is a certain recognizable tone. I've a feeling that you may to some extent have been trapped by your own tone, by its constancy. I've been trying to get out of the stylized language I got saddled with by using the tape-recorder and otherwise experimenting to escape my own style, to use the raw stuff of social reality even as I chop it up and change it around. How do you feel about this?

I've often thought of using a tape-recorder; one wants to lower the fictional threshold. Even if one's fiction is a self-conscious model of existence, one would like the model to have the texture and tone of the original. I wrote a couple of pieces for *New Worlds*, one called "Princess Margaret's Face-Lift". I got a textbook of cosmetic surgery — this was an attempt to lower the fictional threshold right to the floor — and I used the description of a face-lift word for word except I made it all happen to Princess Margaret. But I'm an imaginative writer basically and one writes in a kind of allegorical mode, so that one must be wary of using too many of the techniques of realism. I think they would break the skin of the bubble; mine is an illusionist technique to some extent. If I was a more realistic writer, I'd be more tempted to use the tape-recorder, but for an imaginative writer, one's throwing away one's best tools. Like a beautiful woman hiding her face.

I use the tape imaginatively. I transform the material entirely. I will change the nouns and keep the verbs or vice versa. I'll alter all the tenses and the locality, but I'll keep the tone and rhythm.

I know what you mean: the freshness. I'd like to do that. Maybe I will. But most of my fiction has been straightforward narrative, like *Concrete Island*, or my short stories. All together I've written about ninety short stories, and all but fifteen of them are completely conventional.

As so often in your work, Concrete Island *is a physical, almost geographical representation of a state of mind?*

Absolutely. It's about a man marooned on a traffic island, a man who's already marooned psychologically, before he gets trapped on this island by accident. The island is a state of mind. This traffic island is not the Belisha-beacon zebra-crossing type of traffic island. It's a big triangle of waste ground between and below three converging motorways, somewhere like Westway, surrounded by high-rise concrete blocks. The waste ground is strewn with industrial refuse, old car bodies, all the refuse of post-technological man, and he survives. Quite apart from his "problems", he's within the intense technological landscape, which is an extension of the things I'm interested in in *Atrocity Exhibition*.

Do you distinguish between "pulp" work and "serious" novels?

I don't make any exaggerated claims for myself, but with the great bulk of my fiction, I did my best. With the exception of an early book which I wrote when we were quite destitute many years ago, everything I've written has been of equal value in my mind. I've never sat down to make money from a short story or a novel. I've written what I wanted to write — one must be realistic about this — much of the time within the context of the science-fiction magazines. And it's always been important to me to be published.

Economics apart?

Let me just say that half the stories that went to make *The Atrocity Exhibition* were, when they first went into magazines, never paid for at all. "Terminal Beach" was published in *New Worlds* by Mike Parnell. That was my first "separate paragraph" story, that's where I got the idea from. Publication was the key thing, so one had to write within the context of what was possible. It was lucky for me that *New Worlds* was around when I began.

That conditions the work, not just as an extraneous force but almost internally . . . the completed story lives partly in your typewriter, partly as envisaged in the magazine.

In *a* magazine, not necessarily in a particular mag. I've always been conscious since I started writing that the tide was running the wrong way for the writer, whereas the visual artist, the painter or sculptor, was in a seller's market; the direction of the twentieth century was ever more visual. I sensed way back in the late fifties when I started that the tide was running away from the written word towards the visual mode of expression and therefore one couldn't any more rely on the reader, you couldn't expect him to meet you any more than half way. One's in the arena on the lion's terms.

Eva Figes

Born in Berlin in 1932, Eva Figes is German-Jewish. Just before
the outbreak of World War II she and her family left Germany
for England, where she has lived ever since. She took her BA
with honours at Queen Mary College, London University, in
1953, was married in 1954 and had two children; she was
divorced in 1963. Her first novel, *Equinox*, appeared in 1966.
The following year, she won the Guardian Fiction Prize for
Winter Journey, a marvellous rendering of the mental state of an
old man living out his last days in London, a cross between
"Gerontion" and *Malone Dies* with a form inspired by Schubert's
song cycle *Die Winterreise*.

Eva Figes's book of feminist scholarship, *Patriarchal Attitudes*,
was a success on both sides of the Atlantic, and she has published
several more novels, including *Konek Landing* (1969) *B* (1972),
Days (1974) and *Waking* (1981). She has written children's
books, and has translated and edited many works, both for
London publishing houses and freelance. In 1973 she was
awarded a C. Day Lewis fellowship, and in 1977 was appointed
Writer-in-Residence at Brunel University. The discussion that
follows shows that Ms Figes is interested in rendering specific
perceptions as they register themselves on a flawed sensory
apparatus, and in charting the small but significant movements in
consciousness described by Nathalie Sarraute in *The Age of
Suspicion*. Vividly affected by Faulkner's daring in narrating part
of *The Sound and the Fury* from the point of view of an idiot,
Eva Figes rejects the old-fashioned, normative assumption that
the world appears more or less the same to all of us.

The chronology of her career and several of her remarks about
her working methods here offer some insight into the situation of
a serious writer who is also a mother.

BURNS: *Your first (unpublished) novel,* Lights, *began with your
own birth?*
FIGES: The first memories were when I was three. Some were
only single lines. None was longer than a paragraph. They got
longer as I got older. When I wrote *Lights*, we were living in a
tall house and I had a room at the top which looked over the
gardens. I was amazed at how much I could remember if I just
sat in an empty room, not saying, "When I was three, this or that

happened," but allowing things to come back that I had thought lost. Physical sensations. The sand-box where I played.

Can you recall that now?

At the house where we spent the summer, there was very sandy soil and I was fascinated by the grains of sand, because if you looked at them very closely they were like tiny jewels. I used to collect the grains in a match box. Adults would peep in and find just sand in a match box. I remember to this day that I couldn't understand why they weren't fascinated by these beautiful things.

Did you write Lights *with a view to publication?*

I had just suddenly found a "way in" to expressing myself, and that was what mattered. A way to write that was valid for me. It was a personal, exploratory thing. So although when it was finished I sent it to a publisher, I didn't think about publication very much.

You say you found your "way in". Do you remember the point at which this happened?

I discovered that life was not continuous, that the novels of the past were portraying a false reality.

What about the past, the stream of English literature? Did your degree course inhibit your own writing?

My adolescent interest in poetry continued all the time I was at college. As a student I produced poetry which I now realize was always pseudo-Eliot or pseudo-somebody because I was very aware of the historical processes of literature.

So this breakthrough or "way in" didn't derive from literature? You didn't find a writer who'd done it, like Joyce or whoever?

Certain authors did have a positive effect, but for me there was a definite time lag between study and writing. After leaving college, I had three years of rather serious illness, then a couple of years of childbirth during which everything else was more or less abandoned. It was after the second child was born that I wrote *Lights*. It was a necessary first step, like learning to walk or learning the alphabet. I wouldn't want it published now. It led to *Equinox*, my first published book, a book I don't like now. I used the same fragmented form. I followed a woman through a year. Each chapter was one month, and there were paragraphs in between: things she'd seen, or things she thought, or little actions. In the book, her marriage is breaking up, as mine was. The point was the self-awareness of a woman at a certain stage in her life, when her first youth was over.

Essentially that woman was you?

Yes. I suppose I was cheating by giving it a story-line, though very thinly disguised. The house was one I'd lived in. But I suppose I'd already started splitting myself off, because the husband was not my husband really, though he had certain characteristics of my husband; he was me. I split myself into several bits: the husband was German-Jewish like me, and the woman herself was another aspect of me.

You sound generally unhappy about it.

It's a book I'm thoroughly ashamed of. I don't regard it as really my first book, which was *Winter Journey*. With that book, I felt for the first time that I was really in control of what I was doing. It was a big advance for me, I was aware of that. And I gave it to Secker, and they turned it down because they wanted another book like *Equinox:* an acceptable middle-brow novel, distinguished perhaps by poetic language, but not challenging in any other way. It was a curious situation: the length had something to do with it. A junior editor rang and said, "It's marvellous, you mustn't change a comma, but we can't publish something that's only thirty thousand words." I said: "I'm very sorry but that's the length." Later the reviewers said, "What a gem, not a word too much," so I felt vindicated. But the publisher and booksellers said: "We can't sell this for eighteen shillings."

The book as a commodity.

Yes, a package. At Faber's it was read by a number of people and then sent outside to Anthony Burgess, who said, "Publish it," and that swung it.

Can you tell me about the connection between Winter Journey *and Schubert's song cycle* Die Winterreise?

I'd read Faulkner's *The Sound and the Fury* and was very impressed by it. I wanted to write a book about being old, the defective human being, to write through someone whose faculties weren't a hundred per cent. I connected that with *The Sound and the Fury*. One of my favourite pieces of music was Schubert's *Winterreise*, and one night while I was listening to a lovely recording of it, I thought I could use this form to write about being old. It struck me that the image of the forlorn lover wandering through a winter landscape could be used for an old person, lonely and rejected by society.

So you got the narrative from Winterreise, *but is the book based on it in musical terms?*

No, because I don't know enough about musical form. Music is important, but I'm an amateur. I tended then to believe that, as they say, all art tends toward the condition of music. I envied musicians very much and would have loved to have been able to express myself thus, express pure feeling. I would at that stage have wanted my prose to be as close to music as I could get it.

Do you mean musical in regard to the sound of the words, the form and construction, or the use of leitmotifs, or what?

Construction. Also, I wanted to make a direct emotional impact through prose, to break through the rational prose structures. Also, the indirectness of music, its capacity to hint at things, to say more than one thing at once, which is very difficult to do in prose.

It's at odds with the printing of words in lines. It's the one thing words are not meant to be able to do, and that's a good reason for trying to make them do it.

Quite. It's not pure music obviously, because Schubert's songs have words and music. It's the combination of words and music. In fact, I moved on and decided to use Scott's Antarctic journey as a winter journey within the narrative. I read about ice-floes in the South Atlantic and God knows what, it all seems slightly self-conscious now. I read, for *Winter Journey*, about the ailments of old age. A lot of research is useless, but you've got to know how things work. I used to go through a strange feeling — only the need for a poetic structure could explain it. I would say, "I must find out about stones and geology." I would look at the encyclopedia, or get books out, and I would often not know myself why I was looking. I think it was for the words. It was not systematic research of the kind I've done for a work of non-fiction.

There's a conflict between the research and the fiction itself which has an impressionist quality?

There must be a hard quality in a book, you must never feel, "This woman doesn't know what she's talking about, the tides are not like this", etc. If I'm writing an impressionist seascape, I need to know what all those creatures are called, and what they do when the tide comes in, otherwise how can I create a seascape?

I think at that stage I wanted to create a physical universe, to feel there was something solid about it. Now I've moved into different areas and the gaps are quite important.

Is this related to your wanting to write about the imperfect body or the handicapped person?

This has been a continuing thing with me, though it's changed direction. *The Sound and the Fury* impressed me as having explored new areas of human perception, which hadn't been done before. I chose to work with an old person, because everyone who survives becomes old, it's a common experience, and it hadn't been written about, though by now it's been done by quite a lot of people. I moved on to what I call fallible narrators. We all tend to think of our world as one hundred per cent perception in all directions . . . . We are all defective though we don't think we are. We think of ourselves as gods on two legs, but in fact we're all limited by the perceptions we're born with.

That's a philosophical view. Is there a more personal explanation?

I know that one of the reasons I chose a deaf person in *Winter Journey* is that while I was starting on it I had a bad abscess in one ear. Walking along the pavements one day in the West End, I found that deafness wasn't silence, and this was a great shock. When I put a foot down on the pavement, I heard great crunching noises in my left ear. And this stayed with me and it's in the book. We live in different worlds. The child's perceptions are so fantastically different from the adult's, the sick person's from the healthy.

I get the sense that your work undergoes successive fundamental changes, that you constantly have to note parenthetically, "That's the way it was then, it would be different now." Did Konek Landing *make a big break from* Winter Journey?

I think it did. It's my favourite book, perhaps because it's been unhappily treated by everyone else. I put more into it than into any other book. I felt most about it. Though it was a dead end in some ways, which is why I went on to other areas.

It wasn't that badly treated, was it?

There were a few good reviews, but on the whole people found it difficult and tended to think it was pretentious. I can't speak for other people's reactions. I felt the book wasn't actually difficult to read, but everyone tried to read it too fast. I'd adopted a style such that five hundred pages became two hundred pages with the same content. People should have taken notice of all those commas and read the pages slowly.

You say you put more into it than any other book — in terms of hours worked? Or more?

I got the idea from a very bad television series about a stateless seaman who was known to be about to land and make contact with someone. This is very much tied up with my own background as a stateless refugee from Germany. I wrote out my hang-ups about Germany and the European story in that book. Originally, I thought I'd just write the narrative straight, but I couldn't stand it written that way, it was so boring, and I suddenly saw a very complex narrative. I really pushed language to its limits, rewrote the same paragraph six times, became very conscious of syllables and vowels. I became obsessed with vowels. Somebody asked me if I began to hallucinate when I was writing the book, and perhaps I did, I was so obsessed with vowels. John Berger said, "This book makes a physical impact on you," and that's what I was trying to do.

For me, the vowel is like the piano with the loud pedal down — it has a continuing resonance which sounds beyond the word it's in and creates a sound mood that pervades the whole paragraph. The consonant has the pedal up, makes a single "ping" and is through.

Right. I was partial to open A's. I didn't like E's. I kept looking for words with the right vowels in them because I was so concerned with sound texture.

I still like the book. It had a scope, a breadth of vision, that no other book of mine will ever have. On a personal level, it dealt with the extermination of the Jews. It was a problem I had to solve in a purely personal way, facing up to human cruelty. As an adolescent, I thought: "Yes, well, I'm a Jew, but I'm also a German." My parents' attitude was one of unmitigated bitterness toward the country they'd come from.

When you say of Konek Landing *that you'll never achieve that again, does it make you feel bad, like the rest of your work may be anti-climax? I've sometimes felt that about* Celebrations, *which was the book I put my life's blood into.*

I felt an enormous excitement when I was writing *Konek*. I don't think I'll ever feel that excitement again. But that doesn't mean what I do now is without interest. Maybe it is a little dismal, yes, but maybe that's part of growing older. One has in any case a feeling of diminishing importance about what one does. You accept that you're not. . . .

A genius?

Well, even if you are, it's not important!

Good! You're keeping your foot in the door. Other writers talk of "working something out" through the writing of a novel. The exorcism aspect. Does this work? Did Konek *do that for you?*

Certainly I've never thought about my German-Jewish past again in the way I did before I wrote that book. I didn't realize how traumatic the whole thing had been until my early twenties when I was psychoanalysed, on account of eczema. I once went into the analyst's room, and for want of anything else to say, I told him I'd dreamt I was at Berlin airport and I was taking off and there were all my relatives on the tarmac . . . which was in fact how I left Berlin at the age of six. And he said: "Yes?" And I began to cry. In talking about this dream and weeping, I became aware of my sense of guilt and my need to come to terms with the whole business of human cruelty. So Konek, who is a survivor of the ghetto and an orphan, finds himself in a veterans' home for German soldiers, and this, for me, was going into Hell. The point about these soldiers . . . they were pathetic in a way. I feel that human beastliness is due to stupidity rather than something demonic. It's a failure to understand. And, of course, the soldiers are also victims. This is the central scene of the book, not only Konek's great moment, but the moment when I sorted it out emotionally.

Does understanding the causes of cruel behaviour lead to forgiveness?

Not in the book. Though perhaps it does. Konek goes out of his mind, is found wandering around, ends on an island where he becomes a kind of Christ figure. It's deliberately ambiguous in the book whether this really happens or whether he's still out of his mind. I felt that in the nature of things the only alternatives are to act or be acted upon. The Christ figure is the only way out, because either you hurt others or you get hurt. There's nothing in between. In that book, the main problem was confronting people who have done these cruel things and finding they are other human beings. In the book, Konek not only meets the soldiers who perpetrated all these things, but there is also a man who rapes a girl living in the derelict station. And the way the man talks about the kids he found and this girl, one learns that rape is also perpetrated by a human being.

But writing the book did to some extent enable you to understand and resolve this problem?

The book enabled me to forget the past. It's the past. It's finished. There are certain things in one's past that are like a thorn in one's flesh, and they irritate. This book stopped me thinking about that period in a painful way. It was over.

You said the idea for Konek *began with a television series. How did it develop from there?*

I was making no progress, not that I was worrying about it too much. I usually give myself a rest between books. Then, I remember very clearly, I was coming up the road with the shopping, and I thought, "Well, really now it's about time I made some progress with this idea for a book." And at that minute the whole story came into my head, and I tore upstairs and got out a notebook and wrote the whole thing down. The story line was both significant in itself and quite complex. It was by no means a simple story line, but it came all at once. That's never happened to me before. Usually I fit bits in here and there. And that whole previous year, or it may have been only six months, I had nothing in my mind except cold grey sea and rocks. Nordic landscape, stateless seaman, rocks.

Did it worry you, being stuck on that image?

I don't worry at these problems much. I tend to leave them and come back to them. I think they sort themselves out. On a day-to-day level, if I can't get a thing right one day, I shut the type-writer and go away. The next day, the problem's disappeared.

Do you work regular hours?

Yes, but for short periods. Sometimes not more than an hour a day. I sit down at the typewriter every morning when the children go to school. I work for an hour, perhaps two, but when I get to the moment of uncertainty I stop. If I'm not sure whether to do A or B, I leave it till next day and then I know.

You're working the thing out subconsciously, relying on instinct, just as you did over that longer period of waiting?

Now I can rationalize that particular story, see how it all fits, but at the same time I didn't think like that, I just knew what to do.

So the instinct is followed by the intellect?

Yes, I tend to analyse later.

Photo by Gene Rudzewicz

John Gardner

John Champlin Gardner was born on a dairy farm in Batavia, New York, in 1933. His mother was a high-school teacher of literature who read poetry aloud on the farm, and his literary inclinations were encouraged from a very early age. While still a boy he wrote novels and melodramas. He took his bachelor's degree at the University of Washington in St Louis, and his MA and PhD in English at the University of Iowa. He has taught at Oberlin College, San Francisco State, and the University of Southern Illinois. He has published several volumes of scholarship and criticism on Chaucer, Middle English poetry, and the medieval miracle plays. He is now Professor of English at the State University of New York at Binghamton, in farm country not far from where he was born.

Gardner's many novels include *Grendel* (1971), a retelling of *Beowulf* from the monster's point of view, *The Sunlight Dialogues* (1972), and *October Light* (1976), which was proclaimed the best novel of the year by the National Book Award Critics' Circle. *Nickel Mountain: A Pastoral Novel* (1973), which is discussed at length in this interview, was begun when he was nineteen years old, but did not appear for over twenty years. Gardner has recently become known as a polemical spokesman for old-fashioned values in literature. *On Moral Fiction* (1978) and various provocative remarks about fellow novelists like John Barth and Thomas Pynchon have involved him in a controversy which continues today.

BURNS: *I'd like to talk mainly about* Nickel Mountain, *my favourite among your books, and to begin with what's been called by a writer friend of mine the "Ah!" — the moment the book starts or seems to start, the moment when, as he puts it, "Ah! It's a novel! Or it could be . . ." This may be a tough question, but can you recall that moment in relation to that particular book?*
GARDNER: The "Ah" is a very slow and drawn out "Ah" for me, because I take notes on a story. . . . First of all, I get a very basic idea about what I want to do in the novel and in this case it was a very simple idea. I had a friend who was from New York City who had no experience with upstate New York "apple-knockers", as we're called, and basically he hated them. New York City people are Democrats and my people are Republicans,

New York City people are of different ethnic extractions than my people, and the money that goes in taxes always goes to Albany which then goes back to the farmers, so the city suffers. Basically there's a good deal of hostility between the two. And I like this person a lot and I wanted this person to understand that our people were really not all that bad. So at the beginning of the novel very simply I wanted to think of some typical upstate New Yorkers and go deeply into their lives and follow the same rituals that New York City people go through, basic courtship, marriage, birth of a child, and so on. And that's how I organized the novel. I knew at that point that it was going to be a novel in the sense that I could easily protract the story to novel length.

But I think the "Ah!" really comes when you're working away at the fifteenth draft of the first episode and suddenly a character comes alive — in a way that's quite unexpected, because you create character out of imitation and theory pretty much, but then there comes the moment (as you know perfectly well) when you really are inside the character, in a way you never dreamed you would be, and the words come alive and do things you didn't know they'd do. It's a very mysterious process although it's one that can be taught through exercises and so on. It's a miraculous moment when the character is actually thinking independent of you, even though you are imitating the character the way, say, Shakespeare imitated Othello. You're imitating what the character would say and do, you're thinking about his walk . . . the way you imitated Miss Odekirk in the fourth grade, you know, walking in the hall behind her and doing the horrible limp she had, and so on. But there comes a moment when in your imitation of the character you realize that you're doing things that you yourself would not do. That's a very strange moment, and I think the most important moment of fiction. . . .

. . . *when you've made something and it's beginning to live: one can use extravagant words like "magic" and "miracle" to try and describe it. Do you recall that moment in relation, particularly to Callie, the young girl character, whom I found fascinating? Or Henry Soames, who was equally well drawn?*

I think that girl was pretty lively for me from the beginning. As soon as she started to talk I was on to that girl. I've been criticized a lot – everybody is these days – because I seem to be a male chauvinist pig in presenting women and that really surprised me because I felt that I *was* that character. And of course, if you're sixteen years old and pregnant and have to get married, you're not in a position of much independence. And she's living in the country, with all the country traditions. It would be very strange for her to have a liberated consciousness. But it's certainly true that the minute I imitated her, I felt a kind of freedom. It took much longer with the male character.

Do you keep a notebook?

I used to keep notebooks. It's later gotten too sprawling for that. I have boxes now in which I put notes and clippings, I write myself long essays, and figure things out on paper. The problems in writing a novel, as you know, are terribly complicated. Things like this: you introduce a minor character who only exists to do some very petty thing and then you find you're committed to that character, that is to say, the reader is going to remember that character and you have to bring him back. This happened in *Nickel Mountain.* I introduced a character named George Loomis early in the novel merely because I wanted a sharp and clean contrast with Henry Soames, the hero of the novel, so that everybody would understand exactly what Henry's like, and what he's not like. And George Loomis, in order to perform his function, had to be very vividly created and once you've created somebody vivid and interesting you can't drop him, because the reader is always going to carry in the back of his mind, "I wonder what ever happened to old George?" Then of course you've got to start making up things for him to do, and so on, and the novel begins to take over from you.

Was George Loomis based on someone you know?

Yeah, sure. All the characters I've ever created, if that's the right word, are based on people I knew. The only way I can work is to imitate. Even the dragon in *Grendel,* the monster, the central character, and all the others, were based on people I've known. I thought the only exception in my whole work was in my novel called *The Sunlight Dialogues.* I thought all its characters were imitating specific people except for the Sunlight Man and Clumly, the two antagonists in the novel. But years after the novel had come out, I had been talking to my son, often, telling stories about a beloved uncle I had, Uncle George, and my son when he read the novel years later, said, "Isn't it funny that you used your Uncle George as a model for both the Sunlight Man and Clumly?" And it was absolutely true, and I had not realized it. So I always imitate. . . .

Do you find that your own basic family pattern is inescapable? I mean your family of origin, the family in which you were born?

Right. Your own family's the model of social experience you have. It's what gives you focus on different kinds of relationships and of course if you feel very secure with your family pattern, and if you feel that it works, and since it works, everybody should be that way or more or less so, you always bring that into a novel. But what's also interesting in a novel is to try to understand the people who aren't like you and the only way you can do that is by contrast with that basic family pattern. The family becomes the spectacles you look at everything through. Except in the Hodge family in *The Sunlight Dialogues* I usually don't focus on my own family pattern. I use it to look at patterns that don't work and it's a constant, basic reference.

One thing that occurs to me as you speak is that you analyse extremely clearly, aptly; you have, it seems to me, an extraordinarily high degree of awareness of what you are doing and that results from that combination in you of the creative person, the novelist, and the academic, critic, teacher.

I don't think it comes from the academic. I spent much of my childhood going to Eisteddfods, the Welsh contests in singing and original poetry, and after each recitation or song or after a series of them, the critics would rise and say what was right and what was wrong. It's a very competitive business! The Welsh are thought of as people who get together and sing beautifully. And they do. But they're always thinking about it. From the time you're small, you're remembering this or that critic who said, "When you sing a love song, don't put your hand on your stomach, as Welsh men are prone to do, whereas the Irish put their hand where it's supposed to be, on the heart." Or you hear, "Don't draw out the 'n' in Amen." And because it's so competitive, because you really want to be the greatest Welsh poet in America or whatever, you pay attention. I think I probably went into the academic life partly because it was so easy for me, I was so tuned to thinking in that way. But whereas one kind of academic critic is simply concerned with understanding how things work, my kind of critic, the Eisteddfod critic, is always concerned with understanding how to do the very best. In other words, I'm not interested in just analysing a writer and understanding how he does what he does. I'm always going for the good novel, the one that would win the Welsh contest. Those two things go very well together if they've been in your life long enough, if they're deep enough. As a child I listened to criticism of the poetry-making, so I certainly do not analyse all the time. It's also true that for me it's so expensive in time and energy to write a novel and get it all wrong. I knew a fellow in San Francisco, a good novelist, who got two hundred pages into a novel before he realized that it was unsolvable, that he'd boxed himself in, he'd killed off the only character who could pull him out of the plot, and so on. He actually had to abandon the novel.

I would hate to have to do that because it's so long and arduous. You know, you've spent hours and hours over each page and then to find that two hundred pages, which is a thousand hours, have to be thrown away. . . . It would break my heart.

Though you can learn from some such disasters.

That's certainly true, but I like to anticipate if I can.

Have you never aborted a novel?

Yeah, I have, I have seven novels in drawers that I don't think are worth going back to. Every once in a while I do go back, to remind myself of how I used to write or to figure out how I used to do things because there are certain things that you do as a young man that are wonderful and come easily and other things you do better as you grow older. Sometimes it's useful to remind yourself of how the young man in you did it.

Were those seven novels all early works?

Very early.

So since you've got going, you don't do that any more?

No, I don't do that. Occasionally I abandon a story. But I'm not keen on the short story. I prefer the novel, I'm a big breath writer, as William Gass says, but I sometimes lose the feeling of the story. I start out with a wonderful feeling about it, interested in the characters, and then I get bored and I can't get on with it.

Your books also seem to me big in other ways. They are also big "in time", which is to say they seem to have been written over an extended period of time. The dates by the copyright symbol in Nickel Mountain *stretch in series from the sixties through to the seventies. Can you say something about how that happens?*

I like that method. It's definitely for the art writer as opposed to the commercial writer. I finished my first draft of *Nickel Mountain,* it was a complete and perhaps a publishable novel, and I was nineteen. I published it when I was forty, and I went over it steadily during the intervening years. I would go through it, look for mistakes, fix those I saw, put it away in a drawer, and six months later get it out (meanwhile working on something else) and go over it again and again. I ended up dropping some episodes from the original novel, changing others totally. With each revision I got a gentler novel.

One of the things that happened to me, I might mention, because it's useful to young writers if not to anybody else, is that I couldn't get published. I came along at the moment when realism was absolute master in this country. The only non-realistic fiction was being imported at that time. Kafka and Calvino were first being published in America, in the middle of the fifties – amazing – well, there was some Kafka before that, but very little at a popular level. So I was writing non-realistic fiction and nobody would look at it. And I had written *Grendel*, for instance. Publishers told me, "This is a children's book, and grownups don't like monsters, but the philosophy in it is too difficult for children," and so on, which I didn't believe, and I kept arguing hopelessly. It's useless to argue with an editor, saying that Homer wrote fabulous fiction and so on. Anyway, when I did *Nickel Mountain* I decided I would fool them. I would do an imitation realistic novel and into that novel I would slip ghosts and perfectly impossible situations. It didn't fool them. But in my first version of the novel I was too conscious of editors and too conscious of my rage as a young artist being thwarted by the commercial interests and all that kind of thing. And as I sat on the novel, I sort of mellowed, I lost my ferocious feeling about it and began to pay more and more attention to what the characters would really say and do, what was crucial in their lives and what could be passed over. As I went through it, year after year, I got down, I think, more and more to what is really basic, to what is strong feeling in the life of the country, and its relationship to life in big cities, which is the subject of the novel, which is why I call it "a pastoral novel".

All the traditional pastorals are stories about life in Rome transplanted to the country, to a bunch of sheep farmers, where they talk about complicated issues in simple terms. But as you go over and over a novel the foolishness drops out. There is a great deal of foolishness in contemporary American novels, silly things like – Saul Bellow, whom I admire very much, going on a tirade over some trivial matter. For instance, Saul Bellow was one of those who in the fifties hated Eisenhower. Democrats all hated Eisenhower. He spoke ungrammatically, and so on. He was in many ways a good man and fifty years after the fifties nobody's going to be interested in Saul Bellow's fury at this do-nothing president. It's a trivial moment in an important book, and I think if you sit on the books and go over them you realize that.

There is another matter I wanted to ask about, which is difficult to get at. You touched on it when you were talking about the ease, almost, with which you could describe a young girl character, saying you find the feminine in you, as it were, you find the young girl in you. But over and above that, in connection with the creative process itself, there is the "feminine" in one, the passive, the receptive, which seems to me a key, an absolutely necessary quality in a novelist, particularly because one's got to sustain that act of discovery over such a long period. There's also the "masculine", the bit in you that "makes", actively makes, rather than discovers. Does this make any sense to you?

Yeah, well, I have a tendency to take metaphors literally, but sure, I understand the metaphor. It's true that when you're working on a novel part of you has to sit back and read it over like a sympathetic reader and see if it's true, if it's lovable, if it's moving, and so on, and part of you has to keep shuffling things around and trying for effect. It's certainly true that in the kind of writing I do, which takes place over a long period of time, the most important faculty I have is the ability to be calmly critical. With great serenity, to be able to say, No, come to think of it, a Jewish girl from New York doesn't say, "I feel nauseous," she says, "I feel a little nauseous." It's very important to get every little trifle right. It's important to know what are the real climaxes and what are the false climaxes in fiction, and all that requires a quiet assimilating power, and without it a novelist is nothing.

We have too many novelists who are by that metaphor "all male", that is to say, all "making", and that includes some very, very good novelists. For instance, Stanley Elkin, mainly a short novel writer rather than a novelist, but his imagination is as rich as William Blake's, constantly pouring out all these things but he won't sit back and think it over, and see what's important and what's not. The problem with this kind of writing, I would say this is true of Tom Pynchon too – both geniuses – is that the writing has no climaxes, no ups and downs, no troughs, no levellings. It's just one brilliant image after another until you begin to yawn. It's like a circus act that goes on and on and on, it's thrilling every second of it, but it goes on too long. I think the ability calmly to look it over and edit, and cut, is a wonderful thing. And the ability to see the deep relationships between things. If the masculine metaphor is worthwhile, it would have to imply that a part of the novelist's mind is intellectual, a cold reasoning faculty, making things up which go click, click, click, whereas some of the deepest thought in a novel is symbolic association, the kind of thing that happens way below reasoning. One doesn't know why one's character is like a bear, but one knows that it is, and then as the bear image extends and one thinks about where bears live, and how they treat their children, one gets a deeper and deeper sense of the character.

The relationships between characters, and between characters and their weathers and settings and so on, all of those come from a different kind of reasoning. I would call it left lobe and right lobe: left lobe controlling the mathematical, Nazi side of us, and the right lobe controlling what we call the feminine, the musical. That balance between right lobe and left lobe is enormously important. Interesting, when one starts making biological or physiological metaphors . . . a lot of American writing is anally compulsive, that is to say, very neat, clean, perfectly made, full of bathroom jokes, and thoroughly tiresome. Give me an oral compulsive any day.

You talk of right and left lobe, we could also talk in terms of higher and lower, the area below consciousness, the subconscious, and the "royal road" to the unconscious: dreamland. Are dreams important to your work?

Absolutely, and to an amazing degree. One of my stories, a story that's in *The King's Indian*, is completely a dream, the whole thing was a dream. I frequently have fully plotted dreams, of course any novelist does. I've over and over had dreams directly enter my solutions to psychological and plot problems. *Nickel Mountain* in a way is built around a recurring dream that I used to have and don't have any more. There is a Nickel Mountain. It's a small mountain in middle New York, and it's a very strange place. It's got big mountains on each side of it, it's always in fog, and it looms, and one of the odd things about mountains, as everybody knows who's lived around them, is that they grow, they move, they change. That's not a metaphor, although it's kind of a metaphor, but just as the sun gets larger when it goes toward the horizon, mountains get larger. Sometimes, in the middle of the day, you drive home to your friendly, little, domesticated mountain, and at night it fills the sky, it blocks out the stars. It's an incredible effect. It looks like it came thirty miles closer or grew, swelled or whatever. As a child I had this feeling about mountains, that they breathe, actually, by a very slow rhythm, that the mountain expands like an inhalation at night. This was comforting to me when I was a child, I felt that the mountain was almost human, and God-like, and also a little scary. I didn't like that mountain thinking about me, if it was, I also didn't like it *not* thinking about me, which was really scary. So I had a lot of dreams about being on top of the mountain, with the fog going over, and turning into somebody else, and this became a controlling metaphor.

I think that some of the best things in all novels come out of that. Thomas Mann talked about the parts of his novels that came out of dreams, and there are parts of novels that have a mysterious aliveness that's very difficult to explain. I can't explain it. In some of my novels there are passages everybody points out. I did a novel called *The Resurrection* in which there's a one-page game of blind baseball, a game blind kids play. They have strings around the bases, and a bell on the ball, and they hit the ball, and at one point in the game, in my novel, the ball goes out in the field, the fielders run for it, miss it, and it rolls in the grass and stops. Suddenly, they're all on their hands and knees looking for the ball. And for some reason it's a terribly frightening image. Everybody who's read that novel, that's all they remember! That one page.

Riveting image.

It's a strange dream image. It is, in fact, true: I did see a base-ball game in which that happened, and it wasn't particularly frightening. But I dreamed about it later. That whole novel's built of dreams, of nightmares. A novelist who doesn't bring into the texture, or structure, or feeling of his novel, things that come out of that part of our minds, is never going to be interesting. A mystery writer like P.M. Hubbard, or John Le Carré, is able sometimes to shift into that other world. He's out of the realm of the mystery story, and it's much more interesting. For all our love of Miss Marples, those novels never go into dream, they're always wonderful puzzles and intellectual games, but they never drift off into that P.M. Hubbard country, the *weird* mystery country, or Faulkner country, for that matter. So obviously one must find a way to let that stuff in. If one can't get it in, well, as a serious writer, I think you *have* to do it. Entertainment writers don't. It's probably as well they don't. They'd raise demons that the entertainment doesn't want.

I'd like now to speculate about the kind of novel that you're writing now. I know you're writing one and it's well on its way. Can you say anything about it?

It's titled *Shadows* and it's about an old detective. The book raises what I think is about as fundamental a question as human beings can ever face. The novel opens with a detective aware that he's being shadowed. Somebody's watching him and he doesn't know why. It turns out the person who's shadowing him is harmless, a girl named Elaine Glass, who's the heroine of the novel. She's a wonderful neurotic Jewish girl, beautiful, beautiful heroine as far as I'm concerned. Very, very funny, very sad, very, very bright; a feminist, says all kinds of crazy things, but a lovable girl and very smart. Anyway, she believes that someone is going to kill her, and is moving in on her. She's gone to the police, the police don't believe her. She's gonna get a detective to take care of her and because she's a feminist, she wants a female operative. She's afraid of male detectives, and that's why she's spying on this man to find out – since she can't find a female operative and since he advertises female operatives – she's finding out about him. Gradually the detective, who's an old alcoholic (as all American detectives would be if they drank as much as we're told by Ross MacDonald that they drink), gradually this man begins to believe, becomes sure, that she is indeed going to be murdered. Then, trying to protect her, and in conflict with the police, he accidentally kills somebody, the wrong person, and is sent away to a loony bin. The novel ends with this person out there – the hostile force – coming closer and closer to Elaine Glass, and the detective unable to do anything. That's of course the moment when all human beings pull in God, and that's the only argument for God. We all want to protect our loved ones, who are mortal, vulnerable. And we can't; there's no way in the world. Your child gets a fatal disease, you watch it happen, you do everything in your power, you're powerless. What I want to do in this novel, is, as *powerfully* as possible, to make you *absolutely* love Elaine Glass, and *love* the detective, and *worry* about the society which is indifferent to her problems, and *understand* the religious impulse. That's the overall structure. The problems in working that structure out are all technical problems like: How do you make this girl the most beloved heroine the world has ever known? And this drunken detective an interesting man? And this society which is indifferent to them, not just a "stick-figure" society but a real and interesting society. And what weather is it? What nights does it rain and what nights doesn't it? What does the rain mean? And so on.

That's what I've been working on, for a long time. I've been working on it for about four years (I started in 1974) and I'm not very far. I have thousands of pages of notes and clippings and this's and thats that I hope will help me build that huge cathedral of ideas, but I only have about two hundred pages and they're a pretty rough draft. I work all the time, you know, I work constantly. All day, all night. I type sometimes till I fall asleep on the typewriter. When I wake up in the morning the first thing that comes into my head is what I was working on, and I'm excited and delighted, and I jump up like a kid who's going on a picnic. I run to my typewriter and grab a quick breakfast, which I eat over the paper. So it's not for lack of effort that the novel's unfinished. I figure . . . three, four, five years of this kind of work and going over it and over it and over it and it'll work.

Wilson Harris

Wilson Harris was born on 24 March 1921 in British Guiana (Guyana), where he was educated at Queen's College, Georgetown. He studied land surveying in 1939 and subsequently qualified to practise; he led many survey parties (mapping and geomorphological research) in the interior and was senior government surveyor from 1955–58. He emigrated to Britain in 1959 and began to write full-time. He lives in London with his wife Margaret, a Scottish novelist. He has received two Arts Council of Great Britain grants and has been a Guggenheim Fellow (1973). He has been writer-in-residence at the University of the West Indies and the University of Toronto and has also been visiting lecturer or fellow at many other universities, including SUNY-Buffalo, Leeds University, the University of Texas at Austin and Yale University.

Harris has published two volumes of poems and some short stories, and two books of criticism dealing with tradition and society as they bear on the West Indian novel. However he is mainly known for his novels, which include *Palace of the Peacock* (1960), *The Far Journey of Oudin* (1961), *The Whole Armour* (1962), *The Secret Ladder* (1963), *The Eye of the Scarecrow* (1965), *The Waiting Room* (1967), *Black Marsden* (1972), *Genesis of the Clowns* (1977) and *The Tree of the Sun* (1978).

He discusses the novel in his characteristically metaphorical style, and it is from one of his observations – "If the imagination itself is on trial, then I don't see why imaginative writers whose life depends on the imagination should not speak occasionally, rather than run away" – that the title of this book is taken.

BURNS: *What I'm concerned to get at is the process of evolving a novel, the way the various elements of the mosaic begin afar, and gradually coalesce. I'm particularly interested in the very beginnings, and then in the process of manufacture.*

HARRIS: As you go into this, you will bring in your own element. It will be your eye on certain materials. You want to uncover not merely the beginnings of the novel, but the beginnings that are there before one is conscious that it has or will become a novel?

Absolutely. Is this something you've done before?

No, no, no. I've never done it before, but I think perhaps people should do something like that, because one has the sense

that the imagination is on trial, in a very peculiar way. One lives in a world which has so many things that appear on the surface to be marvellous, technological marvels, yet at the same time we are steeped in such hideous situations, polarizations. . . .

If the imagination itself is on trial, then I don't see why imaginative writers whose life depends on the imagination should not speak occasionally, rather than run away. Writers have this definitive thing of saying, "No, I don't speak about my own work." Deep inside they want to, but they push it under. In some degree that's good, to push it under, but I think this is one time when it's valid to say something.

When you say "the imagination is on trial", do you mean "under attack"?

It's on trial in the sense that people take so many things for granted. They take the objective world for granted. It may be necessary in some degree to come into dialogue with things that lie within the objective world. If you walk down a street, you take the street for granted, you take the trees for granted, but the curious thing is that in a strange way you are quoted into the street. Because people have been living in this place for centuries. They have been shaping it, even the way the trees are planted down there in the street, and in some parts those very old fences could tell you a great deal about what has happened for centuries. People have been conscripted – that's an extreme word, but men have lived in areas of land which look original, but in fact there's a subjectivity written into it by men, generation after generation, century after century, yet people *accept*. They accept institutions like they accept a hill. When I say the imagination's on trial, it means there's an enormous necessity, something crying out from the depth of life, to relate in various ways to the objective world. So that voice behind the novel is not only the very old voice, it's a voice which is aware of the pressures on it. It may be necessary at some times for some assistance to come from that voice. It places a greater strain on the creative imagination because it means that that creative imagination must find a different way of pitching words. His novel truly is complete and everything has been said there. If he is then to discuss it, he must discuss it in a different way, a much more intellectual and critical way . . . I feel all the novels I've written are linked together.

I have that strong impression. Each of your novels is short, you've never written a long novel, yet together. . . . Do you have a "length problem" as a result of your very dense style? Unless one can read the whole body of your work as one giant novel?

There is a continuous development which is a real exploration. You were asking about the beginnings of a novel and I think part of the answer lies in that. There are some imaginations (I don't think all) in which something is building up and building up until it begins to work itself out on the page, and it seems to me the resources are infinite, they are so enormous. So when a particular novel is completed, it represents one aspect of those resources. But there's a development which lies ahead, or which almost looks like it lies behind, as sometimes one goes backward and forward again. Strictly speaking, there is a development which continues all the time, and this has to do with the profound logic of the intuitive imagination: by "intuitive imagination", I don't mean anything vague, it is something immensely concrete, this voice from underneath which is "speaking". One is listening, one is concentrating with all one's resources.

The concentration is to listen, to hear?

To listen, to hear, to move over the landscape, as discoveries are made all the time. There comes a moment when whatever is pushing this thing along retires from the scene, and it will come back again. It retires in various ways. For example, in *Black Marsden,* as the novel moves along: Marsden at the outset seems to have curious powers and then gradually one senses gaps and holes in Marsden, as if he's losing his powers. In fact what is really happening is that Goodrich, who has been guided, taken along by Marsden, has gained all that he possibly can in that phase. So Marsden appears to be fading. Now, there's a misconception, an ambivalence, a difficulty that is written into this, in that Goodrich may misinterpret what has happened. And if he misinterprets, it means that his memories of Marsden would be reduced to the apparent reductions which occurred in Marsden himself. For example, he remembers Marsden as a piece of furniture, animistic furniture. Now this to me has an enormous reality in it because from the outset when Marsden arrives his intention is to bring home to Goodrich the resources that lie under his life that seem to go away into all sorts of other things, that have fallen into oblivion. It's as if as a civilization advances, something has to give way. Cultures have to give way and these cultures are apparently demolished. They fall into the soil. But the bridgehead that comes out of that can only be renewed, can only come out of the institutions that remain to express the advance that that civilization has made. Those institutions can become polarized and animistic in the sense that they appear to have their own soul which is so exclusive that they are unable to relate themselves profoundly to what has gone before. And therefore in some curious way, if those institutions are to renew themselves, they are renewed very often by the very resources that have fallen into the soil. So Marsden at the end appears to reflect the disadvantages which existed at the beginning, when he appeared, as instruments that seemed to have their own soul in such a manner than one can be deceived by their objectivity without realizing how they exploit. As Marsden fades on the way, he is seeking to immerse Goodrich in the elements which could renew his life.

While you were talking about that essential relationship, you were also calling up in my mind a metaphor for the relationship between a writer and his "muse" or his material. I also noted the way you develop your argument — as if there was a hazy map and you were picking your way through it, making connections, taking a small leap, then consolidating. . . . Is that the way you put a novel together, the way you discover the novel?

Yes, I think that is the way I write. That is true to my experience. In *The Secret Ladder,* for instance. When I worked on the Cangi River, a friend of mine was shot. He had taken over from me. There was one man in the crew who was very, very troubled, in a state of anguish. The last week or two I spent on the station, he used to come every afternoon and talk with me. Then I left and this Melville chap took over. He had just got married and hadn't the time really to listen to this man, and the man just came out one day and shot all these people. And I remember getting the news; a day or two after, someone came and said, "Melville was shot." I couldn't believe it. That set off a charge. That issue in *The Secret Ladder.* Now *The Secret Ladder* was not an account. It relates to that, but you wouldn't identify *The Secret Ladder* with what actually happened except that the man Werg is perhaps as close as one could come to the man who shot Melville. (He shot about three men in fact, and another man escaped into the bush.) It's as if that kind of charge is there, written into the soil, and it goes on deepening itself and deepening itself. This is not an intellectual process. At a sudden point it seems to come out, as if the resources have suddenly arrived. Like Marsden, Black Marsden, he's arrived, he's charged! He's charged with some kind of strange wisdom which is revolutionary because what it has at its heart is a new dimension of sensibility. The novel then runs as far as it can go with that kind of intensity and density, as you rightly said, because intensity and density are necessary in that kind of narrative.

Your unique language involves an extraordinarily rapid movement from the physical to the metaphysical, from the realm of idea to the very touchable. The only other book I know that travels at that pace is de Chirico's Hebdomeros, *which is said to "move with the velocity of a dream". This produces a very powerful but very individual, almost private language. Do you agree that this causes problems of communication?*

Yes, as you know, one is involved at a level of communication with something that seems intensely real. And the point is there may be times when this thing could spread itself out in an apparently simple form, but this could only happen as a result of the reality of the dialogue. In my view there is a level of writing which expresses a very deep faith in persons, because one is very involved in something that seems anyway real. One knows from things that happen that that thing is intensely real. There are so many examples one could give of this; let me give an illustration which comes into my mind straight away. This question of the velocity of a dream. The novel on which I am working is set in Mexico, and one of the triggers in the novel has to do with this man we saw on a pavement in Mexico City eating fire. It was late in the evening. Now I won't go into all the implications and associations, but just on this point of "the velocity of a dream". He was standing in the Avenida Reforma, which used to be one of the main waterways that Montezuma rode from one place to another. That whole area was at one time a lake which they built up with dams and piles. The whole area was a lake when Cortez arrived. And many of the buildings are sinking! The Palace of Fine Arts is collapsing, you know? Under the pressure of gravity. Now that is very curious. There's a number of strange things about it. The very word "gravity", which allows one's mind . . . but he was standing on the pavement in twentieth-century Mexico City and underneath his feet would lie one of the sunken canals. Now with the fire going in, he is eating the fire, and one could instantly see this curious man, whatever may have been his torment, one could see in his body, he becomes a clown at one level. There is a religious complication of great density written into his body because the fire that is going into his body reminds one of the sun that used to set on that lake, on that canal, when the doomed emperor was passing, and his mouth as it opens, and the sort of wide-brimmed hat brings back this aspect, as if the man is playing, as if his body is a theatre in which he is once again swallowing the sun. Don't forget these ancient people feared, they had intense fears that the sun would never rise again, that it would descend into a hole in time.

And their fear of gravity, of sinking, is now manifest in their buildings, their Palace of Fine Arts, sinking into the earth?

That's why the place appealed to me. It's related to what I've done before, because you could see in the landscape issues of this enigmatic subjectivity that does not allow you to take that landscape for granted. The same thing applies to Dean Bridge, on which Goodrich stands, in Edinburgh. You may take that bridge for granted, but a lot of people have jumped from that bridge. The water of the Leith is haunted in a strange way by the ghost of Mary Queen of Scots, is haunted also by a lot of people who have committed suicide from that bridge. So when Goodrich stands on this bridge and steps back from the bridge, the car is coming up and he narrowly escapes with his life. The next day when he is walking in the Botanical Gardens he meets Jennifer Gorgon who cuts him dead, as if she doesn't see him, and he is hurt. Because she may not have seen him, on the other hand she may have deliberately cut him dead, you see? He is able to enter into a comedy of invisibility, as if he had been killed on that bridge. If he had been run over by the car, it would have been a further endorsement of what had happened in that place where people had jumped over. But he enters into a comedy of invisibility, as if in fact she could not see him. Written into the bridge are these values that allow him to begin this drama of invisibility. Then he begins this long journey to Nameless. He goes and revises his diary. So you get this self-reversible thing: visibility and invisibility. Now if that is what you mean by "the velocity of a dream", I would accept it. But you do see that the density is related to a profound dialogue with the past which allows one to sense the possibilities of a new dimension, which would allow a society that is hideously trapped in a given place and time to understand that it is not *so* trapped.

That is why it is a hopeful and humanist message?

I genuinely believe a new dimension is possible.

So, to return to what now seems a rather glib phrase, "the velocity of a dream": the question is not the degree to which your work measures up to that concept, but the degree to which it transcends it. The dream world, after all, for all its extraordinary juxtapositions and accelerations, has no past, permits no dialogue with the past. What your perception and style manage to encompass is that which words are not very suited to express because of their linear nature, trotting along after one another in obedient lines. You have, as Joyce did, to achieve this evocation of present and past together. It's as if you should have been a painter.

I believe words can do it. You can have the novel-as-painting (as you can have the novel-as-symphony) and in this new novel I hope some of this will come through. In the novel as painting, it's as if something is bleeding to death, but as the blood comes out, it's light. Now light eclipses light, just as shadow eclipses shadow. Around the object one loses sight of the fact that while there are values within the object, they are values related to the object with the light outside in bands. Those values are completely eclipsed until this object begins to bleed, when the canvas for the first time is taken up by that colour, and that colour reveals the way in which light eclipses light. When you sense that, you sense what values are written into a circumbulature – the alchemical word – the circulation of values going on around an object. That circulation of values we lose sight of entirely because we take the object totally for granted. The object is a tradition in itself. Then that tradition begins to expire. It bleeds. The strange thing is that the tradition is so fantastic that when the tradition appears to be dying, it may be most eloquent. Because as it begins to bleed – it's like a painting – as the canvas picks up these colours, one is suddenly aware of what one has been overlooking for centuries. Now the strange thing is that I believe that words could do this better than anything else.

As you say it, I realize that only words could do it. Their great advantage is the mass of historical association that attaches to each word. Just as objects are charged in this way, words are too.

Just as in your first novel, the one word "Buster". A word is packed with emotion. A word can have opposite values. One could use a word like "tameless" which could mean "free" but which could also mean "ferocious" and "ruthless". "Tameless" could mean freedom, but it could also mean something horrifying. Also the word "nameless". In *Eye of a Scarecrow*, "Idiot Nameless". Now, according to the dictionary, "nameless" means horror, but that is not necessarily so. The fact that something is not named may imply enormous compassion and humility – as in "the nameless unflinching folk". Why does one use that word "nameless"? I knew it was absolutely necessary but I couldn't have given a straight explanation of why I did it. I did not want to tie up "unflinching folk" with any particular group or race of men. Because if a race becomes aware of itself as invulnerable, it is fascinated by that image to such a degree that megalomania could creep in. A terrible animism will grip that people. . . . A rigidity. In other words, they will not have any prospect of a relationship with others. The word "nameless" has to do with what we were speaking of before, the physical world and the psychical world, the dream world. The physical world has its pressures which come in on one. In response, one shoots out into the psychical world to compensate for those pressures. But if one identifies with the psychic world in an absolute way, then one sinks into an idolatry that can be just as stultifying as the idolatry of materialism where you simply invest in what appears to be given. So I believe in the assimilation of these two points in a third direction, which is Nameless. Those two, you name them as psychical and material, but there's a third dimension which is Nameless and that Nameless means that those two are in circulation and give us an opportunity to relate ourselves to the past in terms of a profound dialogue, rather than the simple terms of being derived from the past.

This awareness you call "revolutionary sensibility"?

Yes, it is awareness of a new dimension which one could pick up in various ways. Because I honestly believe deep in my soul that in the heart of people there is the possibility of a new dimension, but this is very difficult to expose because people are gripped from above by the blueprints imposed on them. They are also gripped by the folk thing from below. The tyranny of the family comes both from above and below. So much so that a new dimension of understanding and sensibility can never easily be expressed. And yet this is one of the tasks of the imaginative writer. He can do it in many ways. One way seems to me to be a curious kind of regression, in which you go back and pick up all sorts of signals as if they were signals from the womb.

Pre-natal memory?

And then come forward again. You go back and then you find the point from which you can come forward again. If it were possible in schools of education and sociology to trace how societies regress, it's possible that one could learn how to change societies, because you would have an intimate grasp of what is happening to society, and then you would be able to pick up a point at which you could help that society to move forward in such a manner that it revises itself. Now the creative writer is in some degree doing this in different ways. Another example from a novel of mine, in which there is a dancer who calls himself Caesar, Imperial Caesar. But I remember as a child I used to see dancers like that. They would use all sorts of names: "Augustus", "Attila", or any name, they would use. Caesar I remember. And what struck me, coming back long after, was that those dancers, some of them were limbo dancers, they would bend back and dance under the bar. The limbo dance, it is said, came out of the slave ships. These people were cramped and so on and they began to conceive of themselves as dancing on under the bar that held them. Now the curious thing is that if you go to a country like that (and other countries), people are trapped by historical institutions, let us say, which are imperial in design, they are Caesar's, they belong to Caesar. But Caesar himself was born – the word "Caesar" we identify with the "Caesarean" operation, which is a dismemberment. . . . The emperor and the institutions which have grown up around him which are enormous and sanctified appear to have no connection with the limbo dance on a slave ship. In fact, the limbo itself as it is played in the West Indies today has lost its origins, it's only an entertainment thing, people dancing under the bar, so they themselves are as much locked up in a ritual which is performed for tourists as the man who has now become a kind of fascist, an imperial Caesar. . . .

Now a creative writer with his strange brooding intuition begins to come back, to regress from Caesar, and picks up the Caesarean operation which means the seed of that institution came out of a very vulnerable spectre. And at that moment you pick up the limbo formation too, which is a dismemberment and building up. A genuine creative juxtaposition occurs between the limbo, an anthropological curiosity, and the imperial static thing which is utterly removed from it. When that regression occurs, there is an illumination which allows one to move forward again, because you are looking at the ruling category from an angle which you could not grasp before. And the limbo thing too is re-energized, acquiring a quality it would not have possessed had it remained nothing else but a piece of exotic play.

That is a striking connection between two disparate images; as you say, it illuminates both. When you first make that connection, do you make it brightly, with your intellect, or in the dark?

One of the penalties . . . one makes it half in the dark, half in the light. One has a profound awareness of this connection, but at the time of writing the novel I don't think I could have stated it in such intellectual terms. It was there; it wasn't necessary to state it in intellectual terms. But afterwards it becomes necessary for two reasons: one has advanced into other novels with a development, and one is aware of questions which are asked. People may read the book and miss these connections and then it may become necessary to explain. But it's there in the novel in its creative form. You see what I mean?

I follow you, but a pace or two behind. I'm interested both generally and also in relation to my own work. I make connections which sometimes astonish me and which I have a kind of dumb faith in — literally: I'm unable to talk about it. Is it possible to rely solely on instinct? Do you have to any degree an intellectual understanding of the connection that's made perhaps in the dark?

I think that the connection is there in the work as one is

immersed in it because one is concentrating on the issues . . . the novels you write as well as the novels that other people write, have their own life. They speak to you. Now when that kind of speech is so haunting, that constitutes a development in the novel because the novels of the past are addressing you, are pushed on by things you see, you are astonished at seeing them. In some degree, they're already residing in what has gone before. As you know, and I know this for myself, each novel is a little different, even in texture. Now why does this occur? That in itself I think is of great interest – it's not an intellectual matter – if all these intellectual ideas were there from the beginning, there to me, it's as if there is a chorus. This is one way of putting it, and certain voices are more to the fore, though the other voices are there. Then in another novel, the other voices come to the fore. You have to be attentive not only to what you're doing but in some degree to what is coming back. Because that is also pointing to the future. And one may come to a stage in which it is possible to lay out certain things a little more clearly, or *apparently* more clearly. In my new book, I have a so-called "Editor's Introduction": the Editor is supposed to be the one who is doing the book, but the kind of clarification the editor will enter into is only possible now, put it that way.

You mean this is not a device you could have used previously?

I don't think so, I don't think it would have worked. In fact, as some of the novels are reissued in paperback, I preface them with a short Author's Note. The things I say there could not have been written at the time the novel was written, and yet they are true to the novel! The clarification is something one has earned creatively, by no short cut. I think this is what I understand by development, real development.

Your first book, Palace of the Peacock, *was published in 1960. How do you feel about it now?*

I feel *Palace* was my first authentic book . . . one discovers things in odd ways. For example, *Palace* has running through it constantly this preoccupation with music, which I could not explain philosophically or emotionally when I wrote it. In fact, at some stages I was worried by it. Because most critics will tell you this is wrong: "Stick to the words, the word is the tool." But deep down within one's life, one knew that something was authentic. I attempted to set this out in a diagram, with the Caribs. The Caribs were locked and liberated at the same time, within a theme . . . they would eat a morsel from the bone, then make the bone into a flute, and when they performed this they were riddled with hallucinations of all sorts of contrasting spectres: the rock, the child, the mother. So . . . when I speak of music, I'm not speaking of song, I'm speaking of the *action* of the music, rather than the sound it makes. I'm speaking of music as if music acts, as if the bone of the flute penetrates through different spaces. All these walls, you know? Each wall, each horizon, represents one area in which the imagination is locked, which it seeks to break through in order to pick up another element. Therefore one has a theme of community, an annunciation of community. Because it moves through the Feather of a Bird mask, into the Rainbow, into the Black Marching Boots. Now that's hideous, that's the assault. But that breaks again into the sharp wings of the Butterfly, the Forest becomes the Wave of the Drunken Boat, Eldorado, all those journeys across the ocean and right into the heart of that continent. And now the danger with twentieth-century man, the danger with the current thing is the animistic side. At the animistic level, they're simply seeking the absorbed energies of the opposition by devouring it. If the enemy came, if they could eat a morsel from the enemy, they could learn all of his secrets. In other words, there was an enormous hubris planted in this scene, that was very dangerous. That is the death wish. Because they are doing something that is impossible they will die attempting to do that. And they did: the Caribs have disappeared. If one looks to the latent side, to different horizons and spaces, you could have a community in which, rather than being overwhelmed by catastrophes, you could digest the catastrophe in degrees. That means one has the capacity to survive as a creative organ . . . you see what I mean? So in a novel like *Palace* . . . there was this rapport with the past, not started intellectually because I didn't know it! I've done this research afterwards. This business of the bone, the bone that sings, and the bone that sings because it faces these skeleton walls that are implacable, and they yield this capacity to break and mend, so that an architectonic scale comes into play, quite different from the static thing one has been educated to respect as the sole criterion of art. Because I've always been taught that stasis is the supreme criterion of art. I do not believe this. In reply to your question about *Palace of the Peacock,* it became for me an important novel, because it is the first apparition which comes out of these resources.

You talk of catastrophes, the decay of societies, the fall of imperialisms; this suggests the marxist concept of contradiction and things containing their own opposites. But you made a passing reference to what you called "the idolatory of materialism" which seemed a gesture of contempt. . . .

I'm not contemptuous of marxism, but the way marxism is taught is quite horrible because it's become a frozen object. Whereas I would have thought that the very spirit of Marx is enormously creative.

I feel that one is in dialogue with the sacred. I use the word "sacred" in a very special sense, to imply that there is no escape from a dialogue with something which could be very oppressive in this universe, or could be very liberating, depending on how one enters into dialogue with it. Now when values start eroding as they are eroding in our age, we are aware of enormous oppression, but that may be because we refuse to see that we are being summoned to come into dialogue with all sorts of eclipsed horizons. Now I do not believe that this runs contrary to the very depth of Marx. But if one were to go into a school of marxism now and speak of the dialogue with the sacred, as soon as one uses the word "sacred" this is a religious thing . . . they wouldn't want to hear it . . . except those who are unusually keen and sensitive.

Nevertheless, your view contains elements of marxism?
I think so.

How do you feel about reviews? Is there any critic or other person whose opinions of your work you respect or value?

Most criticism is on a very quick level. *Scarecrow* was very generously reviewed by Burgess, and other critics were interested in it, particular aspects of it fascinated them. But the problem for me anyway is – and I think you would sense this – the whole problem of what one means by values. This is one of the reasons why I think it is useful to speak about the novel and so on.

I have been simplifying my own style, using tape recorders and the rhythms of ordinary speech to find a new simplicity, connect with people in a way that I'd lost. Are you worried about the degree to which your work is understood?

I think what you have done is fascinating, and it may spring in a strange way out of the direction your work has been taking, because your novels have been taking a path deeper and deeper into the disorientation of the world, the post-war world. The essence of what you're saying is that you are looking for certain rhythms, within. Those rhythms could constitute something which in my own vocabulary I would call a new dimension, if you could sense how those rhythms relate to areas in people's lives that are not usually related at all. To come back to your question: for myself, I have always felt – you may call it naive – that my novels are not as difficult as some people would say. That is probably naive because people find, say, *The Age of the*

Rainmakers, very difficult. I don't see why. But still. . . .

Wilson, haven't you just demonstrated to me, in the range of reference and the kinds of connections you are making, that they must many of them be individual to you, and to that extent private? I know I can enjoy and understand your books without necessarily following you in every connection you make.

I must say this: I have always felt that many novels written and instantly accepted could be very difficult novels if they were placed in another context. In England today, many writers have a solid back-up coming from friends they know, coming from schooldays, coming from universities. They meet and talk about the issues they write about, many of the critics write about the work of their friends; it doesn't mean they will always praise the work, but it means they understand it in some degree. So they have that kind of back-up, and back-up has to do with values. Now it's true that . . . I've been for a long time immensely haunted by the ghosts coming from English literature and in some degree I share that side of things. But my curiosities in Britain are probably a little different from the curiosities of many English writers. For example, with Margaret, my wife, I find many things in the Scottish area which are very curious and which people never comment on at all. One has a Gaelic tradition, one has a Scottish, it is a heterogeneous thing; people will say of course that Britain is homogeneous, but it doesn't seem so to me. And apart from that, with these other connections we've been discussing . . . one does not have easy back-up, you know? It takes people a little time to correspond with the kind of thing we've been talking about. But there has been no other way for me: I've had to work through all of this. But I would say some of the novels are less difficult than others. *Black Marsden* I would certainly say is a less difficult novel than most people think.

Whether or not it is, does it concern you?

It concerns me in the sense that when you write so deeply, you instinctively believe that it is a valid communication. Valid communication is working with all the resources – you cannot put them aside. So if the thing comes out in an apparently simple form, it is because those resources want that simplicity.

That's another instance of content governing form?

It's an aspect of what you would call the daemon of the imagination which has a fantastic purpose. "Private" or however you choose to express it; that's not the right word, though I use it myself sometimes. That kind of demon is far wiser than you or I am. Therefore there must be some reason why one has to work with that kind of concentration and . . . truth to what one sees. It may issue out in something people say is simpler, but in fact, is it? A painter like Cézanne, is he simple, or not? In one sense, he seems tremendously simple, it's a staggering simplicity. But what does one mean when one says that?

I think the word is not "simplicity" but "familiarity". If I pick out and use the rhythms of contemporary speech, it isn't because I think they're simpler than your dense prose style, but because they're more familiar and therefore more acceptable.

Strangely enough, you put your finger on the thing which may perhaps explain something that is purely psychological for me: I find I go into a place that is utterly familiar and it becomes unfamiliar, as if it points in two directions. One you might call the road of science and one the road of art. The road of science has all the names written up, the other is the way of art, which is the ways in which science itself is subjective, so that that road seems to be going into the unknown. Now this is absolutely true; this is a psychological experience I have had. Suddenly, the whole place is turned around. The unfamiliar place seems to be familiar and the familiar place becomes utterly unfamiliar.

That's a marvellous experience, literally. It transforms walking down the road.

That happens to me in these London streets. I come to the end of a road and I'm suddenly astonished. The road is leading to an abyss! Honestly! And then you make a tremendous effort and you tie it up.

In a different degree: I am acutely aware of the earth beneath the city, its essential contours and its ancientness. Nevertheless, what you're describing is of much greater intensity.

It has "the velocity of a dream". It forces one to discover all sorts of things. I've discovered, for example, the underground rivers in London, which I never knew of until recently. Not far from us here in Holland Park, an underground river runs. There are several rivers like that, I know of six or seven. The lake in Kensington Gardens, you know? That's the surfacing of a river. . . . I got this book on the lost rivers of London, which are actually running underground. Some of them come up in people's basements. And sometimes ghost stories relate to these rivers because of the swish of the water sometimes people seem to hear . . . movements that could have come from the waters. Men who work on the sewers, they would know of some of those rivers. So those rivers have been devastated and trapped, and they take their revenge, people are suddenly —

Given twinges?

Given twinges.

John Hawkes

John Hawkes, born in Connecticut in 1925, was an ambulance driver with the American Field Service in Italy and Germany during the latter part of the war. He then returned to Harvard University where he took Albert Guerard's creative writing course. Guerard almost immediately got James Laughlin of *New Directions* to publish *The Cannibal* and "Charivari", both of which came out in 1949. In 1947 Hawkes married Sophie Tazewell and they have four children. Anyone listening to John Hawkes will be struck by how important Sophie is to him, not only as a wife and inspired editor but also as a kind of muse. He often says, "I married Sophie and began to write," in a way that implies the two events were intimately connected.

Since his fast start, Hawkes's reputation has continued to grow. *The Lime Twig* (1961) and *Second Skin* (1964) are probably his best known books and have been widely used in American university literature courses. His other novels are *The Beetle Leg* (1951), *The Blood Oranges* (1971), *Death, Sleep and the Traveller* (1974), *Travesty* (1976) and *The Passion Artist* (1979). He has also published two books of short fiction and several plays. Theatre, especially Shakespearean theatre, is important to him; *The Blood Oranges* was written with *Twelfth Night* in mind, and *Second Skin* plays with *The Tempest*.

In spite of his very high critical reputation (he has been referred to as "one of the half-dozen authors of first rank in America today", "one of the very best living American writers", and so on), Hawkes has never had a bestseller, and has continued to work, first for the Harvard Press (1949–55), then as a teacher of writing and literature at Harvard, Stanford, MIT and elsewhere. He joined the faculty at Brown University in 1958 and is a Professor of English there. He has maintained his lifelong friendship and respect for his early mentor, Guerard, and this is connected with his belief that teaching is an important calling. He clearly thinks of himself as a teacher and a writer, not as a writer who has to teach for a living.

The power of Hawkes's writing lies in his images – images of incomparable vitality, vivacity, humour, contrast. They carry the weight of his novels, or, rather, they create the structure that bears the weight. He says: "I began to write fiction on the assumption that the true enemies of the novel were plot, character, setting and theme. And having once abandoned those

familiar ways of thinking about fiction, totality of vision or
structure was really all that remained. And structure, a verbal
and psychological coherence, is still my largest concern as a
writer." He goes on: ". . . related or corresponding event,
recurring image and recurring action, these constitute the
essential substance or meaningful density of my writing. . . .
However this kind of structure can't be planned in advance but
can only be discovered in the writing process. The success of the
effort depends on the degree and quality of consciousness that
can be brought to bear on the fully liberated materials of the
unconscious."

Nathalie Sarraute describes the novelist's greatest obligation as
the discovery of the new, and avoiding the crime of repeating the
discoveries of predecessors. John Hawkes uses similar language,
and he puts his money where his mouth is. He talks of writing "in
order to create the future", and says: "Any fiction of any value
has about it something new. The function of the true innovator or
specifically experimental writer is to keep prose alive and constantly to test in the sharpest possible way the range of our
human sympathies and constantly to destroy mere surface
morality."

Hawkes's talk is funny, but unsettling. His matter-of-fact
assumption that all is fictive, that there is no *mimesis,* no
grounding, but only a choice of floating islands in the void, still
startles. His reading of the father's suicide from *Second Skin*
provokes laughter, but the most nerve-racking laughter imaginable. People who preach the uplift value and moral guidance of a
literature founded on some stoical acceptance of "reality" are left
gasping. Others who have read the latest books on innovative
fiction get a vertigo-inducing sample of how it feels to *live* on the
floating island that many critics only write about.

What follows is not so much an "interview" as part of a floating
event before various audiences at the University of Minnesota.

HAWKES: I'm an obsessed fiction writer. Really. I'm obsessed
with such things as horses, dogs, birds, sexual destructiveness,
lyricisms, children. . . . We all know the Jungian archetype of the
child as totally vulnerable and totally invincible. None of the
children in my fiction are invulnerable, they're all maimed,
injured, harmed, killed, punished in one way or another because
I think the children in my fiction actually represent the writer
himself and the list of maims suffered by children in my novels is
really quite impressive. . . .

In *The Beetle Leg* a little boy dies of a snake bite. In *The Lime Twig*, a little girl is shot by a local constable. (That's what constables are good for, shooting little girls.) In *Second Skin* the protagonist is given his daughter's fetus in a fruit jar as a birthday present. In the novel *Travesty*, a little girl is the victim of a hit-and-run driver, who is actually the narrator of the fiction. So they don't fare well, but on the other hand they are in some way or other necessary to the fictions and I'm interested in them.

The first little boy appears in *The Lime Twig*, and quite fortuitously *The Lime Twig* is a novel set in a mythical England because I had not been to England when I wrote the novel. This novel is about a young man and woman, very young people who are married, Michael and Margaret Banks, who are really very old people, old and dead, probably at the end of the Second World War. They have a lodger called Hencher. These two young people, Michael and Margaret Banks, are destroyed by a cosmic horse-racing gang. The member of the gang who really causes their destruction is William Hencher, their lodger. Hencher is a great fat man (I'm also obsessed with size, largeness, fatness, missing it myself except in the wrong places). Hencher lives with these people and he has only three ways to love. He loves his dead mother. He loves a little boy he sees every morning, for some reason, fortuitously, and he loves finally by getting Michael and Margaret Banks out of the flat and taking Margaret's lipstick and drawing great red circles around his eyes and lying on their empty bed and simply loving. Some people would call such a character perverse. I think he's the true lover and he begins the novel in a prologue, and his description of the little boy ends with the words: ". . . love is a long close scrutiny like that."

For me this fat, poor narrator, who is finally kicked to death by the horse that destroys Michael Banks's life along with Margaret, is really talking about the creative process. I think that love is exactly that kind of scrutiny, and I think that fiction too is a scrutiny as well as a constant constructing. That scrutiny should always be there.

There's also a dog in that novel. I've never owned a dog but I once saw such a dog, after Faulkner died in Virginia. It was raining and the red clay was wet, and this fat dog came from nowhere and crawled to me and I knew that somehow he was the figure out of the novel I'd already written. It is the scrutiny of the flesh itself, of all which is non-existent, that's important.

My novel *Second Skin* is narrated in the first person by a fifty-nine-year-old ex-Navy lieutenant, junior grade, called Skipper.

He is an artificial inseminator on a tropical island, and the novel was written in the Caribbean. I'd gotten pneumonia in Providence, Rhode Island, where I teach at Brown. Providence is of course the sepulchral city, that's why I like it. It is dead and empty and barren and cold and I got pneumonia. And the pneumonia was marvellous pneumonia and as a result of it a poet friend of mine gave us a ten-year-old guide book to the paradise isles of the world. And I opened it up and came right to the page about Grenada which is down near Trinidad. Sophie and I and our four very young children took off for Grenada which turned out indeed to be a paradise except that we didn't want to meet any Americans and of course as soon as we got to this place, and it was the furthest we could get from the United States, with the money we had, who walked down the beach, a beautiful little crescent, absolutely innocent and mythical beach, but two figures obviously American, recognizably American from a great distance because the man was wearing an enormous cone-shaped hat the colour of brick and the woman looked like George Washington and they said in unison, "What are you doing here?" And I said, "I'm going to write a comic novel about suicide." And suddenly the beach was empty and we had our paradise isle to ourselves and I wrote a novel about suicide, and the narrator, Skipper, is living as I say on this wandering tropical island and his father of course was a mortician who committed suicide, and I think that Skipper's wife committed suicide, his daughter committed suicide; it too could be called, I guess, an obsession except that I do want to say strongly that I'm very opposed to suicide. At a certain moment in the novel, Skipper recalls his effort, when he was about a ten-year-old child, to try to prevent his father's suicide. The father, the mortician, is sitting on a lavatory seat, in a bathroom, with a pistol and a box of ammunition in his hands, and a child is going to try to save the father's life by playing his cello, which is what Skipper did when he was a child, clearly another sort of allegory of the artist at work.

When I wrote that novel the one real purpose I had in mind was to be sure that I would write a novel that couldn't be mistaken for anything except a comic novel. It is a comic novel. The writing of this fiction was the most pleasurable of any writing experience I've been in. As I've said we were on a tropical island and every morning I would sit up on a veranda with dark glasses looking out toward the sea feeling like a criminal, and life was very pleasant; the children were often at school and there was nothing but the light and trade winds, sea, and then writing in the morning and every afternoon. I can't swim but I could float. So I floated in the water to try to wash off the filth that had accrued in the morning's writing. Finally there came Christmas vacation, so suddenly the four children were all back and I had to have a place to work. The man and woman who owned the plantation provided me with a workshop or studio, a combination pigsty and dog kennel, made with cinder blocks. It had a tiny room with two windows without of course any glass; by this time the real nature of paradise had been working on me so I had marvellous sandfly wounds on one shin and they had spread and grown and were suppurating in a wonderful fashion. In the little room where I sat trying to write, really quite happily writing, there was a table and a chair and nothing else. A little bird always came to this window that looked out towards the sea, never to any other window, and I always could see the bird, and watch every once in a while a ghostly ship pass by on the horizon, obviously with nobody on the ship. The walls and the ceiling too, which was most remarkable, were covered with little lizards, sort of made of green rubber, all over, thousands of these little green lizards. I have a particular fear of small creatures yet they were somehow comforting, a kind of rug carpeting of little strange creatures. I would put my feet up on the rung of the table but the ants were more numerous than the lizards. There were armies of ants in that little room and they knew exactly which leg of the table to climb and they knew how to make their way finally to my sandfly bites so that in a sense the whole process was completed.

I resist and resent very much the idea of associating research with fiction writing. It seems to me a bizarre incongruity to even think of researching something which is real in order to create a fiction which is a fiction. On the other hand, this narrator had to be an artificial inseminator (and it was with this novel that I achieved a kind of sexual breakthrough: there's not really any sex between people) . . . I needed to know what the process of artificial insemination was really like. So one day when the artificial inseminator appeared I walked over and stood by him and it was the greatest disappointment imaginable. Artificial insemination itself is a very banal idea. I mean this young man was wearing a black suit, carrying a satchel like a physician, he was utterly bored. He took off his jacket, rolled up his sleeve and inseminated the cow who was just as bored as he was. It only took a moment and when you think that what he was actually doing was depositing inside that remarkable enormous animal the seed of some bull worth millions of dollars in England — because obviously that's where the seed for insemination would come from in the Caribbean, from that great lovely dying landscape of

England — well, it was a disappointment [*laughter*]. But every day, between writing and floating, I used to go down from where we were living to a field where the great Brahmin cattle collected, and there was a kind of feeding trough there filled with sugar cane and these Brahmin cattle were enormous and made as if of stone, and their heads must have been four or five feet long. They were altogether prehistoric. I was not afraid of them actually. I went in among them and got as close as I could to these great mouths salivating over long long strands of sugar cane. And the mixture of saliva, horns, nostrils and sugar cane, sweetness, life, well, it was a very remarkable experience and nothing's equalled it since.

Ever since the writing of *Second Skin* I've had a very hard time coming up with what to write about, which is very painful. A few years ago at any rate we, my wife and our children, were in France, in Brittany in the summer, and I was there to spend the year to write a fiction, but I didn't know what to write. I ended up writing a novel called *Travesty* which is very short and I think has a very interesting, in a sense, genesis. It started with the idea that we'd actually transported ourselves through lovely France. I speak not a word of French, or any other foreign language. . . . At any rate I had nothing to write about and for some reason or other there was a copy of Camus's *The Fall* in English. . . . when *The Fall* was first published in this country in about 1956 in English translation, I opened it up and read one paragraph and I remember saying to myself, I will never ever write a monologue, what a boring form. So of course I found *The Fall* and read it and suddenly found myself thinking terrifying thoughts about Camus because I thought at the end of his life that he had fallen into the pit of Christianity which I simply couldn't understand, it was painful to think about. . . . One day I happened to witness an automobile crash that could only be conceived and acted out by the French. It was the holiday season, the time when French families would come to Brittany with their children for the sea and so on, and I saw in a narrow little black tar road near the beach two very small and extraordinarily fast automobiles coming towards each other head on, both filled with parents, children, picnic paraphernalia, umbrellas and all that, and they crashed head on, and at that moment it was simply extraordinary because everything disappeared. I mean that it was so scattered, the debris, that there was nothing left of the accident itself and that suddenly made me think that I had had an idea of what I would write and it did bring to mind Camus and I had the idea, an erroneous idea, that Camus died when he was driving a car at night in the rain with a young woman companion. That was what I vaguely thought of Camus's death which was totally wrong. At any rate I realized, I knew immediately that I was going to write a first-person novel that would imitate the form and the actual length of Camus's *The Fall*. But it would differ from *The Fall* in that I had not read anything, and still haven't, of Camus's philosophical essays but I had gotten the idea that Camus had said we cannot live unless we can answer the question "Why not suicide?" And it suddenly came to me that the way I would write the questions that would fill my novel would be: How suicide? Where suicide? When and why and what can we do with suicide? So the novel is a monologue spoken by a nameless man who is driving a very fast, a lovely, beautiful car through a southern French night with his best friend seated in the right-hand death seat. His best friend is named Henri, he's a poet. In the back seat of the car is the narrator's daughter Chantelle. Henri is the lover of the narrator's wife, and also of his daughter Chantelle. The real reason I tried to write the novel was to try and write about what was unimaginable and the only thing I could think of which was really unimaginable was of course extinction or death or annihiliation. So this is a comic novel then in which the man in the right-hand seat is a poet; and ever since my youth when I was unable to write poetry, I've really wanted to do this to a poet [*laughter*]. The narrator is driving the car with his passengers through the dark night in order to crash the car against a three-foot thick wall of an abandoned farm house, and the reason he's doing that is, as I say, to try to make himself and the poet experience and actually imagine the end of life. It's important to know that the mother or wife has a tattoo and in one of my novels I had a scene that had a lot to do with grapes, real grapes, but in this novel, this woman has a tattoo in her erogenous zone, below her navel, a cluster of marvellous purple grapes and they figure in the scene. There is a reference to Apollo in the opening lines and the narrator says that he doesn't know why Apollo's there and I didn't know why either. I wrote the novel on a child's pad that had on its cover a big naked archer with a golden bow. The narrator also recalls his one other child, a little boy named Pascal who died at about the age of three. So in this death drive, the narrator is proving to Henri that he, the narrator, is not simply crazy or inhuman. And this is the only passage I've been able to write in praise of the child.

The last agony for me of writing came about last year when again I had nothing to write, really. Great depression, lovely depression, was seething all over the place and then there were a

series of fortuitous moments. I remembered a passage from my
first novel that had been written thirty years before which is to
say, of course, if you suddenly run out of gas you simply go back
and start over again. I remembered a passage about a group of
women who went into an insane asylum in order to put down a
riot. And I remembered the source of the paragraph. It was a
story that my father had told me when in his youth he'd been a
member of the National Guard in Connecticut and had volun-
teered to go into a women's prison in order to put down a riot. I
remembered that the National Guardsmen at that time were
armed with barrel staves, and somehow, the story, the moment
came back, of my father involved in this terrible, terrible outrage
and I realized that I would try to write a novel about a riot in a
women's prison. The really important event was when I was at a
conference having to do with literature in southeastern United
States, or southwestern United States, it doesn't matter where.
There was a critic, who no doubt was a structuralist. He was so
infuriating and I felt so debased in his presence that I realized
that I had my protagonist. This novel, called *The Passion Artist*,
is about a middle-aged man named Conrad Vost, who lives with
his daughter, a very young daughter. He's a widower, in a
mythical Central European town that houses the women's prison.
The reason everybody's there is because of the inmates, and
Conrad Vost's mother has been an inmate in this prison for years
and years because of murdering his father. Little Conrad Vost,
when he was a child, in his little white dressing-gown, saw one
evening his father entering the farmhouse wearing a nightshirt
and carrying a knife. This man had been exiled by his wife to live
in a store room. The woman, the protagonist's mother, has a
kerosene lamp and she's about to light a great big stove with
some fuel in a can and the murder occurs when she sees her
husband, turns from the stove, flings the kerosene, the gasoline,
or whatever it is, on the man, breaks the lamp and sets him afire,
turning him into a lovely human torch. Luckily there's a lot of
snow outside and he rushes out into the snow, tries to keep from
dying, but of course dies. After that event, little Conrad Vost
lives on, and a lot of this novel is about what is going on in the
unconscious of the protagonist. Little Conrad Vost was sent to a
farm for disordered children where he first learned, or tried to
learn about love from a horse while dissecting the genitalia of a
mare. The woman who runs the farm is called Anna Kasulski and
she drinks a lot of wine and is a brutal woman and one day she
tries to seduce little Conrad in the presence of Anna Kasulski's
assistant whose name is Kristel. Kristel is a very young woman,

really a little girl, and Anna Kasulski is actually trying to seduce Kristel but she's not successful. Kristel is aware of this sort of travesty performed on the child so the next night she goes to the child and leads him off on a sort of trip, or a sort of moment of love, and this is my idea of lyricism, it's not really comic, but it's lyrical, I think. It starts: "Come with Kristel, whispered the voice in the night. . . ."

I read Travesty *with some pleasure but to be honest I wasn't quite sure how to approach it. . . .*

The novel has to be read in two ways: As a realistic fiction with a genuine suicide murder occurring, but it also has to be read as the process of imagining and as in effect the acting out of the imagination. (I know this because of the young German woman in the United States now who is writing a book on post-modernist irony in American fiction and last year she was working with Barth in Baltimore and now she's working in Providence with me and that's the way she describes how to read *Travesty.*) The idea, it seems to me, is simply that as the narrator, who is of course the poet, as the narrator approaches the very moment of extinction, he is imagining more and more. He is imagining with great ironic pleasure, nice pleasure I think, wholesome pleasure, he's imagining he had a chest X-ray that day, and he's imagining how some clumsy fellow with one of those French cigarettes that I would so love to smoke had I not given them up years ago, how a technician will look at the lungs, will look intelligently at the lungs of a man already dead and the novel is simply filled (it's a short novel, I can't say filled), it alternates between moments of in a sense fictive reality and moments of what the narrator imagines and of course they're indistinguishable. When the narrator describes the actual crash of the car, it's really a better accident than the one I saw in Brittany.

In Travesty *there's a vivid scene in which children get stung by wasps at night. Did that actually happen?*

While my work is very personal, my fiction is not generally autobiographical at all. I hope that wasps actually can't fly and sting at night, I felt they couldn't, that's why I put them there. I live a peaceful, kind, tender life. But there was one awful moment on an Atlantic island. . . . There was a little cottage in a nasty little pine grove with enormous rocks like gigantic skulls as high as the room, and one of our children went into a little clearing and stepped on a wasp's nest. He began to hop up and down. His brother and sister rushed in to try to save him, and they hopped up and down. I was horrified, standing there watching my children trying to save each other while being stung to pieces and I was remembering how my mother, in my own single childhood, had tried to save my own skinny little body from the pain of wasps' stings, by plastering it with mud. I was so self-preoccupied that these two experiences coincided until finally I did exert what could be called my will. I went in and brought all four children and carried them out and got one nasty sting which pained and infuriated me for days.

How do the shadows of war and events like Three Mile Island affect your writing?

I think that we live by our imaginations. I think there are few really important subjects. I used to say "human consciousness, the imagination, and woman". But we strike off woman because to put woman as one of our crucial subjects is to mystify her and we certainly know that by now woman must be de-mystified. I haven't been able to do that, but at any rate I think we live by our imaginations and a sense of strangeness, and have been for how long, I don't know, many many years. We're surrounded with not imaginations but mimes, if you can call them that, mimes that are really bent on destroying it all, obviously. If once we realize that everything is a fiction, which of course it is . . . I'll grant a concreteness. . . . But we are living imagined lives which we imagine. And if we don't know that there are people whom we believe as being real and accept as real instead of recognizing them as fictions which we should destroy, well, they will of course finally manage to put their marvellous schemes into effect, put a grid of nothingness on us, and we will be extinct. And I really do think that the most important human faculty is that of imagination which is always trying to create something from nothing. It is an irony that destruction really means nothingness, so in one sense perhaps we should be ready to welcome it when it comes. Sophie, my wife, gave me a little card once and it had an epigraph of Georges Bloch on it and the two lines were simply, "The vase gives shape to emptiness, music to silence." So obviously, we exist, we come from our context of nothingness, space and silence. And anything that is other than space and silence is, in a sense, what we create. I can't help but think of fictions as artefacts created out of always the nothingness and always pointing toward that source of zero, a sort of zero source. That is why for one reason among others I so admire John Barth, because the more elaborate the fiction gets, the more you create, the more you know exactly the nothingness it inhabits. Paradox is the second word, after imagination, that's most important to me, and, well, the word "dignity". That reviewer who called my work the work of a contemptible imagination didn't realize that of course every act of trying to write a fiction, no matter how violent it may be, no matter how horrifying it may seem, obviously what it involves is the dignity of the faculty we have of being able to imagine.

You talk of nothingness . . .?

The void, the void, the absolute absence of anything. One of our children is in computer science and for years I detested computers and science, and computer science etc. He is a very creative person and he gets very irritated when I say science is just a fiction that creates out of stuff, things that we can work from. It's all fiction. He says, "Dad, you're crazy, it's all real." He has tried to teach me a certain sense of science. He tells me life exists other than on this planet, and I say, "Huh, what nonsense." And he says, "It has to." Then I can only think to myself: "If it does, it's only contributing all the more to the void." Have you never had that terrible sense, suddenly, that you don't know who you are? Or why you are? I've had these experiences all my life of being aware of how it could come to be, and whether it's going to end in any second. I'm very interested in the ending and I find that lots of younger people are not. They say, "Oh, well, I wrecked my motorcycle yesterday and nearly died and it didn't mean much to me." I say, "Well, death does mean a lot to me and I keep trying to imagine it."

One of the things that's hard about beginning to write is the self-exposure that's involved. It's dangerous, it's embarrassing to publish the things that you've written and I wonder if there comes a point when you pass that?

When I began to write fiction, I was an undergraduate at Harvard, but an older one, because of war. I began to write fiction simply accidentally, one summer. It was a wonderful summer, when Sophie and I got married, I began to write fiction, I went back to Harvard for my last two years and met Albert Guerard and got in his fiction-writing class and finished the short novel I'd begun that summer and wrote *The Cannibal,* my first novel. In the next couple of years I worked as an undergraduate with Guerard and I certainly was not concerned in any way whatever with the notion of exposure. This was a small undergraduate writing class, it was very vicious, in a sense, it was very real, nobody was worried about hurting anybody's feelings. I was married, and in that class, and very soon my teacher Albert Guerard said that my work was going to be published and got it to the publisher of *New Directions,* James Laughlin. . . . So in a very few months, my whole life was formed and pre-determined. I was simply excited or totally unbelieving at the idea that this work was going to be in print. This was in the Fall of 1947, there were still many veterans in college, and we were all older, and there were about a hundred and fifty people trying to get into Guerard's fiction-writing class of twelve and I was one of the people admitted to the group. The first meeting of this fiction-writing class was for me a moment of tremendous anxiety. It was in an old Harvard building in a classroom in which the teacher was not only on a podium but there was about a six- or eight-foot stage, a "judges' box". There was Guerard up there and I had noticed somebody else come into the room, another student wearing a trench coat. . . . Then the teacher started the class right off by saying, "Well, one of you has already written work which is simply going to be published." And I thought, "That guy in the trench coat." Then Guerard said, "I'm going to read aloud a few paragraphs of this work," and I heard my own words coming from his mouth, and was overwhelmed. .

For the next two years, everything I did and lived for had to do with Guerard and Sophie, and these were marvellous times. Writing *The Cannibal* for me, a first novel, was an exhilarating experience and an unselfconscious one, we lived in two very small rooms and friends would come by and it was perfectly normal for Sophie to be talking in one of these small rooms with a friend and I'd be in the other room that had only a bed in it, so I'd have to lie on the bed trying to write my novel. I wrote it all the time. I took a lecture course on poetry, and I wrote quite a lot of fiction, in the back of the notebook, instead of listening to the stuff about poetry. Phrases and images constantly came to mind, I wrote them on match covers and things. That novel came out in a sense preformed, I knew I was in total control and very happy because of Guerard's support and not worried about exposure; the thought of being published, even though he said it, at the outset, didn't really dawn on me until finally Guerard arranged to have Laughlin meet us and Laughlin said, "I guess we'll bring out this book and. . . ." He spoke in a very casual way and Sophie and I went off. . . . We didn't have any money, but ate a steak and we were very, you know, excited by what was happening.

Since then I haven't really ever been worried about, "Have I exposed myself?" through a sentence that I would just as soon change. Or maybe very, very infrequently. For instance, in *The Blood Oranges*, the woman used the word "baby" all the time. I took out hundreds of "babies" and the manuscript of the book still has too many of them and I'm sort of sorry for that, but nothing serious. I don't think I've ever failed myself really seriously as a writer so as to want to revise, to change a book that's already been published. The matter about being exposed is a double edged-thing. The work has to be made public. I feel lots of anxiety and hostility about the critic who talks about my contemptible imagination. I am the kind of person who is looking for constant acceptance and support, and love from the world at large, which I rarely get [*laughter*]. I'm a little anxious about my novel *The Passion Artist,* because for the first time in my life I found myself wanting to respond to a topical idea which had to do with women. The man in the novel is the most vicious character I could create, the person who knows least about women, etc. The women in the fiction are treated pretty badly and I just hope by the end of the novel it will be clear that I'm not actually a misogynist. And the cruelty in the fiction is what I think helps to produce a lot of the power of the language, if there is that power there. But there is more to it than that. The most surprising moment for me as a younger writer was after *The Cannibal* was published. I had graduated from college a few months before, and I was working in a little book store of the Harvard University Press. A man I had met in a writing class came to interview me for the *Harvard Advocate,* an undergraduate magazine. He was trying to model his interview on *The New Yorker,* which I knew nothing about, and his first question was, "How does it feel to be a writer?" I did not know what he was talking about. It had never occurred to me that I was a "writer". When I began to write, I had no idea of the role of writer and I never wanted that role. Recently, it's been creeping up on me, I have to sort of accept the idea of somebody saying, "Well, what are you?" Well, I teach, or I write. Or I am a teacher, or I am a writer. But I detest the signs or the garb, the preoccupation, the self-preoccupations, the tallying up of reviews, the wearing of strange, flamboyant clothes to make it perfectly clear that you're not only a writer but a very important writer. That's what you are. You're a writer. You may be a father, you may teach, you may have cousins, you may have a wife but it's being a writer that's the most important thing. I loathe this whole business. It should all be done in secrecy. Somebody said, a really lovely idea, "Allow us to do our work, but none of it should ever be published. There should be a time limit, twenty-five years, fifty years, before it's ever seen by anybody." That's not such a bad idea, well, it is a bad idea, because the work is being produced at a certain time and has to have, or it's trying to have, its collaboration with the reader who exists in the same time. And I have to admit that I would like to have more readers and I think probably there are more people reading my fiction now and there will be still more soon.

Although the responses may be even more vitriolic than before.

I'm reminded a little bit of that scene in Hemingway's Moveable Feast *in which a writer and his wife are having this quarrel and she launches at him: "You . . . you . . . writer!"*

That's a beautiful story, and I agree. Being the wife of a writer can be a pretty odious thing. Say the man is a writer, the woman's collaboration is never really acknowledged, yet it's extraordinary, and the fiction could never have been created without that particular collaboration and it goes unadmitted. I have just read *The Real Life of Sebastian Knight.* Sebastian Knight lives for six years with a woman named Clare. Clare not only loves him, but the important thing is that her imagination is like the writer's imagination and the narrator says, "No wonder Clare fits so well into Sebastian's life." That's not what people living together are supposed to be doing, simply one of them fitting into the other's life. It's perfectly clear in the novel, despite Nabokov's humour, that he is pointing out the kind of terrifying total usurpation of energy, time, space that the writer sucks from the person living with him and it is a very destructive thing.

Do you set aside a certain amount of time every day for writing and do you do that rigorously?

I don't generally try to write fiction when I'm trying to teach, and I've been fortunate to have gotten enough grants, and been able to take off time to write. I think trying to write is real agony and of course a great pleasure, all at the same time. I don't keep any journals or notebooks and I no longer find myself hearing phrases that I can write on the inside of match covers and I don't carry the matches anymore anyway. No notes, no note journals, nothing saved. If I have an idea that I'm able to begin to try to use as something to write a novel out of then, yes, I would begin to write at eight o'clock in the morning and try to write three . . . if I write three hours now I'm very lucky. It used to be that I could write about four hours but last year it was getting to two and a half hours, I was not able to stand the prolonged effort to shape sentences the way one wants to shape them, and I am a writer that does not write lots of drafts. I have revised two novels extensively, *The Lime Twig* and *The Beetle Leg,* and after the first draft they required an awful lot of re-assemblage, reconceiving and sentence-by-sentence revising. But since *Second Skin*, I have not done any kind of serious revision and maybe I should have, maybe that's a problem, but as I try to write, I'm doing my best to get the sentences coming out pretty much as I would like them to come out, in finished form. I'm trying to hear the novel that I would like to read, so I write very slowly and actually in a pathetic, very sophomoric sort of way. I count words because I feel I can write, say, six hundred words a day, which is two pages, more or less. If I'd written nine hundred words that would be extraordinary. Then there were days, as I was beginning to finish the novel, when I would be writing up to almost four pages a day. But generally speaking, I would write a very short amount each day, but at an absolutely prescribed time and in circumstances that are precise. Always the same, always the same table, the same chair, I write with a pen on schoolchildren's tablets, not legal paper, there's something about the oversized yellow legal paper that puts me off. I like the idea of a children's tablet and up to now Sophie has typed all my work. I read it aloud to her, then she makes comments and I might try doing some handwritten revisions as I write. She would type the first draft, then she would read it, marking it up, then I would respond to her marks, then she would type it again. We've finally gotten to the point where we've been able to afford a typist so that my wife doesn't have to do all this typing and the next time that I try to write a novel, which is going to be the year after next, I've decided that I'm going to try to do my writing in the morning by hand, then I will try to type it myself in the afternoon and try to spare Sophie this work, although she'll still be reading it and commenting on it.

I've never written a novel in which I've known where it was going to go. I've had the beginning or the ending, but never the actual direction day by day of a plot, so for me writing always has a risk, and risk is a word that's important. As you begin to try to conceive of a fiction and try to write it you are involved in terrific risks, which gets back to the fear of exposure. I think I'm not afraid of exposure but I know there's a lot of risk in exposure. I am by now capable of bearing it, either being overlooked or being vilified. I know the quality of my work and I actually knew it from the beginning. As soon as Guerard told me what its quality was I believed him, and from then on knew it. The mechanics are like that. On the other hand you know there is always a kind of pre-conscious thinking going on, hopefully. For the last several years that's been happening to me less and less. That is: while using the electric shaver I haven't found myself imagining, seeing scenes or hearing words. That was when I realized that nothing was happening when it should be happening. I began to get worried, but in the last two years I have been thinking about fictions, conceiving scenes and for the first time I have an idea of what I want to write next. Even a beginning, and an end, and the characters, what it's going to be about, hopefully. *The Cannibal* came about because I saw a *Time* magazine article about a literal cannibal, it was a very short paragraph. In Berlin they apprehended a small innocent cannibal and the idea suddenly of eating . . . appealed, it set me off. Within a few days of reading the article, I was trying to read a book called *The Last Days of Hitler,* and I learned that a friend of mine had been institutionalized. So, here I was reading about Hitler, thinking about a cannibal in Germany and thinking about a friend who had been hospitalized for emotional reasons, thinking about my own days of hospitalization, and suddenly the novel cohered and I knew I was going to try to create my own post-world-war Germany, a sort of reconstruction of a ruined Germany, and that a Nazi would be the protagonist. I knew at the outset that I had to reverse my own sympathies, that was the whole point of the novel, to think, to be in the person of the victimizer, rather than the victim. Not to be maudlin, I think from my earliest days I probably had some strange sense of myself as victim, whether it was asthma, being too thin, too short, too shy, too whatever. You know, I've been a kind of victim person. When you write fiction of course you become the opposite, you become the authoritarian, the authority, you are in control of everything. My fiction has always depended on the relationship between unconscious conflict and a conscious shaping or controlling of this stuff.

That's how *The Cannibal* got started and it took exactly nine months. It was an easy novel to write and was a pleasure to write although I was writing it in alternate time sequences. The novel is set in 1914 and 1945; I was writing really in alternate sections and when I was done Guerard said, "This book would be too difficult to read, it's absurd, take all the 1914 sections and put them in the middle so that the novel has three parts." Which I did. I've learned since of Faulkner writing *Wild Palms* and *The Old Man,* and claiming to have written sections of these two novels alternately. As his energies would flag on one novel, he would turn to the other, to get his energies going again. I don't know if that was happening to me or not. It's simply that I had to have a contrapuntal structure so that I could shift realities, quickly, constantly. I couldn't stay in one world very long.

The Lime Twig was written because I read a newspaper article about legalized gambling in England. I was so appalled at the idea of a country making money on the dreams of its population that I wanted to write about that. I've loved horses ever since. . . .

B.S. Johnson

B.S. Johnson was born in 1933 at Hammersmith and, except for his evacuation during the war, lived mainly in London until he took his own life in 1973. He did his Honours English degree at King's College, London University, starting at the late age of twenty-three. He was the author of seven novels: *Travelling People* (1963), *Albert Angelo* (1964), *Trawl* (1966), *The Unfortunates* (1969), *House Mother Normal* (1971), *Christie Malry's Own Double-Entry* (1973) and *See the Old Lady Decently* (1975). He also published two volumes of poetry, and two collections of short fiction, *Statements Against Corpses* (1964) and *Aren't You Rather Young to be Writing Your Memoirs?* (1973). He was a prolific writer, director, and producer of films and television; his 1967 film, *You're Human Like the Rest of Them*, won prizes at two film festivals. He was poetry editor of the *Transatlantic Review* for ten years, and wrote several theatre scripts, including *One Sodding Thing After Another* for the Royal Court.

Johnson's novels are carefully crafted and formally experimental without being flashy. He was influenced by Beckett, as can be seen from his film, radio, and television work as well as from his fiction. And he was a powerful spokesman for the right of British writers, indeed the *need* for them, to try whatever formal innovations they thought would prove interesting. He himself published a novel (*The Unfortunates*) which consisted of unbound gatherings of pages in a box, allowing the reader to choose the order in which to read them. But, somehow typically, he hedged the bet by designating two gatherings as the beginning and the ending, setting a limit to his experiment, and a limit to how much control he would relinquish. And the subject of *The Unfortunates*, a deeply moving book, is the death of a friend, which has been an occasion for writing almost since humans began writing. He was willing to try new things, but was also devoted to the novel as high art, to being "a novelist of quality".

JOHNSON: All my novels started from a moment – usually a very pleasant moment – when I said: "Ah! *There* is a novel! I can make a novel out of that!" The process of writing is a confirmation of that moment of recognition, and so far there's never been a moment unconfirmed. Whether I make it come true or it

was true in the first place, I don't know.

BURNS: *Do you have to wait for these moments to occur? Are there periods between novels, waiting for it to happen?*

Since I started writing in 1959 I've had to earn part of my living in other ways so there's always been a backlog of novels, sometimes two or three, waiting to be written. I've just finished a book, and now I'm working on a trilogy.

Can you recall one of these initial moments?

Not precisely. With *Travelling People,* my first novel, it must have happened in 1959 when I was working in a sort of drinking club in North Wales. When I returned to England in September of that year I'd had the idea for the book, though it was another two and a half years before I finished it. During that time I had ideas for two more novels which became *House Mother Normal* and *Christie Malry.* In between, three autobiographical novels, *Albert Angelo, Trawl* and *The Unfortunates* forced their way in, demanded to be written out of sheer personal need, psychotherapy if you like, though I call it exorcism. I wrote those three books to get them out of my head. I wanted to unburden my mind: "It's not in my mind: it's over there, in a book." Those books were written to relieve that kind of pressure.

I know The Unfortunates *commemorates the death of a friend. I can understand your need to exorcise that memory. Does each book have a similarly tragic background?*

Basically yes, but I hope they're witty, moving and poignant nonetheless. *The Unfortunates* is an extreme example. In *Trawl* I explored my sense of isolation, my failure to make lasting relationships. I wanted to define this isolation and thereby understand and ease it, in the classic way.

The memory or feeling you wish to exorcise: what form does it take? A nagging thought? Recurring dream? A headache?

It's a preoccupation. It takes up more time than I'd wish, more than I can cope with. I know by experience that writing does the exorcism job very well. I was looking at *Trawl* the other day, and there were things in it I don't remember having written, don't remember having happened.

You write not to clarify a memory but to obliterate it? Or, by clarifying, obliterate it?

Obliterate is the wrong word. I want to change its form so I can refer to it voluntarily. If I want to recall how I felt at the time I wrote *Trawl* I can read *Trawl,* but I don't have to carry it with me, I don't want that stuff popping up in my mind when I've got better things to think about.

You want it on the shelf?

To distance it, not obliterate it.

Once you get the idea for a book, what's the first thing that goes down on paper?

I carry little notebooks around, about three inches by five. I buy them in Paris actually, for sentimental reasons. I make notes about things I think pertain . . . things I want to write about, things I think are useful for these novels I have in mind. . . .

I bung these notebooks into a drawer and from time to time, when I'm incapable of anything else, I do a filing job. I prefer to write, but as you know, everyone has times when they can't write and that's when I do the filing. I tear the pages out of the notebooks and stick them into folders marked with the names (or until they have names, the numbers) of the novels I'm going to write. Some notes are indecipherable because I was drunk at the time, or writing on a train or whatever. I always think I'm going to transcribe the notes into a book within a few days, but it's usually years.

Do you, like me, make notes almost in an absent-minded fashion, they almost take you by surprise?

They do occur unexpectedly. I get them down in recognizable form as fast as possible and then get on with whatever I was doing before I was interrupted. They're what Joyce called Epiphanies, sudden moments when one realizes there's something worth writing down. Something clicks in my mind and I know I must do it. It's a common experience. I'm pretending I'm not unique.

Very rarely do I note down the words that actually go into the novel. Often it will be a phrase that only has meaning for me, a personal shorthand to recall what I saw or heard. What goes down in full is a rhythm, if a particular rhythm takes me. There are all sorts of rhythms stuttering away in my head, which I like to keep with me. Rhythm is the most important thing to me.

It's a musical thing rather than a meaningful thing?

I don't go as far as you on that, they're equally important. The balance in English literature swings from one to the other. Dylan Thomas went towards music and after him it went flat and concentrated on meaning. Just as Bach combines sound of fantastic beauty with technical mastery, I attempt a combination of form and content in which neither dominates and both are in harmony. It's arguable whether I've ever achieved it but that's my aim.

Do you note down images or ideas?

Essentially they are pictures.

Something seen? Or remembered? Or dreamt? Or imagined?

All of those, though I don't dream much. I may see something, or something comes into my mind that has passed the filter of memory, and thrust its way to the surface, for reasons I've never understood. That's what *Trawl* is about. *Trawl* is an extended metaphor for the way the mind works. The trawl goes down into the sea and you don't know what's happening as it drags across the sea bed, or why it comes up, until it comes up.

Trawl has a physical shape that can be drawn on paper: *Trawl* begins with a prologue, followed by exposition, then development, reaching the highest point in the novel: then it explodes, disintegrates, falls down into coda. The design is a line.that climbs a steep incline, then falls at a sudden point, then collapses. This was drawn on paper by a Hungarian critic (the book was translated into Hungarian) called Georgy Novak. The shape of the book's construction is the shape of a trawl: it drops quickly down, travels along the sea-bed and is slowly hauled to the surface.

It's also the shape of the keel of a ship?

It's the shape of the first half of the book, the reminiscences.

It's a fantastic theory. What do you think of it?

I don't think about it at all. I feel: it is there. I don't know how significant it is. The book has an inner consistency which I don't remember putting there consciously. I don't know how the book happened. I just know it's right. The subconscious of the mind, all the myriad impressions one's ever had, is like a vast sea and this little net dives down and pulls things up at random.

There is, down there, a mass of useless junk mixed up with things of value: how do you distinguish the good stuff from the bad?

Empirically, by whether I use it or not. There's some wastage. At the end of each novel there's always a pile of material, bits of paper not used, which goes back in the files, available for future novels. I don't throw anything away. The house is overflowing with bits of paper.

Is the overall construction of the novel dictated by these early fragments, rather like those pictures made of dots in kids' comics? Do you join the dots up?

Yes, but they don't dictate the overall structure, which is after all a very simple thing: beginning, middle and end. I start by sorting the bits of paper, seeing which bits go with other bits, exactly "dot-to-dot", it's a good image. Accidents, like the order in which the bits got thrown into the folder, often dictate juxtapositions which weren't there by design.

I then sort the papers into a series of other folders which represent the sections of the novel, according to a previously thought-out structure. Some sections are quite long, others half a page, others a couple of lines as in chapter twenty of *Christie Malry*.

The second stage I call starting to write the novel proper. It can take two or three or six months or a year, but it's relatively the easiest part of the book. The exact timing is partly decided by economics. Even as personal a book as *The Unfortunates* had to be written on time, as the second book of a two-book contract with Secker. The key stage is finding the form. That happens between the first idea (the "Ah!") and the filling-into-sections I've just described. Between those two points I work out the form suitable to the material I have in my mind plus the stuff I've got down on those bits of paper. It was at that stage I settled on the book-in-a-box random form for *The Unfortunates*.

How do you find the right form?

I rarely sit down and work it out, it goes on in my mind. But having "done" English literature at university, having read the work of many modern writers tackling similar problems, I have a compendium of possible forms and I select one, by a process of mental trial and error. The bits of paper with notes on do not influence the choice of form. Each bit is like a brick in a whole house: the house is built of bricks but they don't dictate its architectural form.

You've described your subconscious as the main source of images and ideas. What part does your conscious mind, and your awareness of social and political factors play in the making of a novel?

Outside writing I'm a very political animal. My novels have generally been written from a political stance but the politics have been very much in the background. The books have mostly been concerned with other things, like the nature of writing itself, its relation to me, not to other people or society.

Is there a split between your political and your writing self?

Definitely. I've wondered about it and been concerned about it, though *Christie Malry* had a definite political viewpoint. I disagree with socialist realism: "You must write things that people can understand and you must write things that help towards socialism." That I reject utterly, not because I'm not a socialist but because I am. In England I don't think books can change anything. Here if you want to change things you've got to throw bombs or work through Parliament. Three years ago I went to Hungary and many Hungarian writers said, "We envy you your ability to write whatever you like." But when they wrote something their government didn't like they got thrown into jail. In England no one takes a blind bit of notice. Writers are no threat to established British society.

And whatever you wrote you could not make yourself a threat?

I think those short films we made for ACTT had an effect, however tiny, on the fight against the Industrial Relations Act. We helped a bit in mobilizing the trade union movement.

Isn't it tragic that you are unable to mobilize your most powerful talents? The heart of you as a man goes into your best writing but you cannot harness that power to the service of your fellow man?

It's my fellow man's tragedy as well as mine, because he's not been brought up to receive whatever I have to give in the form in which I'm best able to give it. They don't regard books as a way of changing the world. I'm talking about our contemporaries, not the generation of, say, Welsh miners who educated themselves in libraries, reading Marx and Lenin, nor of the Left Book Club in the thirties. There's nothing like the Left Book Club today. So I don't write for political reasons. Maybe I'm a writer because I'm no good at anything else. I may be no good at writing either, but I couldn't do anything else. I have a simple need to express myself, not a need to have what I write read by others.

You write like Malone writes? It's a kind of excreting and there's no point in explaining it, it just happens?

That's the exact image. I just know it's something I have to get rid of.

Forgive the question, but does writing help you resolve questions about identity?

Not for long: *Travelling People* gave me an identity in 1962 but not in 1972.

Do you type or write?

I type at the very last stage. I work from those bits of paper in longhand on to loose-leaf lined quarto sheets. Sometimes for shorter pieces I work in manuscript books in pencil. One draft balloons into a second and is worked over again and again and again. It gets interspersed with poems that occur while I'm working on a novel. A novel gets so complicated, with chunks of prose changing position, that I have to work on loose-leaf. When I've done all I can in manuscript it's ready for typing.

[Reads Mss] Pity anyone trying to type from that! It's a fantastic network of interpositions and interpolations, all arrows and re-jigs and re-thinks and editings and crossings-out — all in very swift soft pencil. Pencil keeps pace with the speed of your thought?

I like the graphic quality of pencil, I like the way it looks.

I do the editing job with scissors, cutting up the pages and spreading out slivers of papers on a large table.

I haven't the room for that here. I sometimes use scissors if

Virginia's typed the stuff for me, but I usually type for myself. I learnt typing at fourteen. I failed the eleven-plus and went to commercial school where they taught me shorthand, typing and book-keeping. Useful. While I'm typing I can't revise, I can't think. The manuscript gets into such an involved state because I have to do all the creative work before I start typing. Typing a novel becomes more depressing and painful every time. With *Christie Malry*, though it was short, I was bored stiff, not by reading it because I wasn't reading it, but by the mechanical act of typing.

When the typescript's finished who do you show it to first?

My wife. I never show anything to anyone while I'm working on it, not even to Virginia. I may ask her about the odd word, but it would be a very minor thing. My marriage doesn't work that way, Virginia's never set herself up as a literary critic. This started with *Albert Angelo*: I showed her the manuscript and she didn't know what to make of it. I was very disappointed. It was the first time I'd shown her my work, and that she didn't see how good it was (in the way I thought it was good) was a great disappointment.

Were you only seeking praise?

Confirmation that I'd done the right thing.

You didn't want an informed critical reaction? Only confirmation, even congratulation?

That's common in writers. But my showing the manuscript matters less and less now. It was important that *Christie Malry* was finished on time, for economic reasons, there was a feeling of relief about that. Virginia didn't read much of that book, it wasn't the right time for her to read it, though I wanted her to like it, I wanted very much for her to find it funny.

Is there anyone else, publisher, editor or agent, whose early opinion you value?

From an economic angle obviously one's publisher's editor is very important. If he likes it and praises it, apart from agreeing to publish it, that's a bonus. My first editor, at Constable, was very good. He took *Travelling People*. He spotted some weaknesses, though this was a year after I'd written it and I could see them for myself. He was good for me, but he was sacked not long after the book was published. As to critics, I have to ignore the bad things people say about me, otherwise I wouldn't write any more. Some people are simply trying to stop writers writing. This is a common thing with people who have no creative ability at all. It's an old cliché but that doesn't make it less true. The thing they'd like above all else would be to stop everyone writing because they can't do it. For myself I can't allow either adverse criticism or praise to change the way I write.

So there is no point at which the writing process is completed by your obtaining a definable reaction?

There isn't. There was with *Travelling People* and, to a lesser extent, *Albert Angelo*. I used to rely on this man, Tony Tillinghurst. He looked at the first two novels and improved them by his suggestions, he acted as a rein on my self-indulgence. He died of cancer and it's all recounted in *The Unfortunates*. Since then I've never trusted anyone enough, no one at all.

Have you tried to create a new relationship to supply this need, or is it a need?

I find I get on all right without. The nearest thing was my editor at Collins, Philip Ziegler, who talked a lot of sense. With *Christie Malry* he made a few minor suggestions and one major one. In the book a group of young revolutionaries discuss how to make war on society: "We could attack the clubs!" one says. Another replies, "Yes. The Atheneum!" Then in dialogue they named every club in England from the list in *Whitaker's Almanac*. Philip Ziegler said it was boring, he thought it didn't work. Now I have some sympathy with anyone who says that that was a piece of self-indulgence. But I like lists and I think I have the right to be self-indulgent sometimes. But I chopped up the list and made a few other jokes, about Pratt's Club, The Reform Club (which is a joke), and Bucks. . . .

I understand your feelings about lists, they have an absolute quality.

Yes, the totality of the list.

Why is one drawn in that direction? Were you wrong to give in? Did you make the wrong kind of compromise? Was Ziegler's rationality making a quite proper interposition, telling you to stop when you should stop?

There are many historical examples of this thing about lists. This is not something we have invented. There's that enormous long list in *The Odyssey* of all the ships that went there, all the places they came from, just a bloody list.

Is there something of the ritual about it, something incantatory, like a drum beat?

Yes. I like lists. It's a poetic thing. A list implies that you are including everything, it's an absolute, an attempt to impose pattern on the chaos, it's all sorts of things. One's following Beckett, he likes lists. There's a lot of it in *Watt,* and in *Molloy* where the guy on the beach changes the pebbles over, he goes through *all* the possibilities.

And in Murphy, *the guy with the biscuits, deciding in which order he should eat them.*

Yes, very funny. Sometimes Beckett plays a joke by making a deliberate mistake to catch you out.

A list also makes a joke of or comment on traditional narrative: "Nothing's happening and it doesn't matter." A list in narrative terms may be said to go sideways, or stay still, it makes no narrative progress at all.

In *Albert Angelo* the teacher calls the class register and I put in the whole thing, with every bloody kid's name. A straightforward novelist would have written: "He called the register."

And be glad to have left it at that. Very sensible. Whereas the complete list drives the reader mad. Is that a good reason for doing it?

For me the act of writing is a way of not becoming insane. Life is chaos, writing is a way of ordering the chaos.

Can't writing reflect the chaos by becoming part of it? Disconnect to the point of irrationality?

Even *Babel,* your book of chaos, is fixed, it is not chaos in its own terms. The images you have juxtaposed in a particular sentence are there for ever. You don't reflect chaos, you use a metaphor for chaos, because you create a new order, in a fixed pattern.

Are you ever deliberately inconsistent? In Celebrations *I say a man's got blue eyes and two pages later they are brown. I've done it purposely and I know it's right, though I don't quite know why. Do you do this?*

I would tend to use it as a comic device. I've done it with characters' names. In a short story, "Instructions for the Use of Women", I wanted to tell what bloody happened to this girl but because of the laws of libel I couldn't name her. So each time she appears she has a different name.

That's a naturalistic justification, but the purely arbitrary is not for you?

I think it should be done, but not by me. Like many of your things, like *Babel,* I'm glad you wrote it because it saved me having to do so.

My going so far out on a limb was partly made possible by the backing I got from John Calder. I felt he respected my work and (consequently?) I respected his judgement. That relationship was built up over many years, but you have gone rather swiftly from publisher to publisher. Has that had an adverse effect on your work?

The trouble is that one has to have an economic as well as a literary relationship with an editor (what he thinks of your book means money) and the two things don't go well together. And however nice a guy the editor is he never seems to have the power to put his judgements into practice. Some money man, for irrelevant non-literary reasons, interferes with the money or the publication. Ideally, in a small firm, a sympathetic editor would also make the financial decisions.

What about other writers? For example, we've known each other for years but this is the first time we've ever talked about writing.

As poetry editor of *Transatlantic Review* I know a number of poets and I talk or write to them about their work. I went down to Port Talbot recently to do a poetry reading with a poet called John Tripp. We talked a lot about writing and hardly at all about money. He wrote me later saying that unlike other English writers I cared enough about writing to help a fellow poet. That happened in Wales. In England writers rarely help each other; it's a great pity. I don't discuss the novel with other novelists because I have strong notions about what the novel should be doing. Most novelists disagree with me and I am not in the business of converting them to my point of view.

Are you in the business of learning from their point of view?

No. I did that in university, studying The English Novel and reading hundreds of them. I've done that bit and come to a position where I am right. If they can't see it then the strength of my case is such that they haven't properly understood.

You're right for you, while they may be right for themselves?

Right. I was with Anthony Burgess and someone said, "Why don't you talk about the novel?" He said, "I don't want to talk to Bryan about the novel: he has views about it." He had his own ideas and he didn't want me upsetting his apple cart. I have never found anyone to debate with on the subject. When I sit down to write a bloody novel I've got to make certain assumptions about the function of the novel now and in relation to every novel that's ever been written. No one can write the same after *Ulysses*. *Ulysses* changed everything. But people do write as though *Ulysses* never happened, let alone Beckett. These people simply imitate the act of being a writer, a deliberately anachronistic act, like writing a five-act verse drama in Shakespearean English. So there is nothing for me to discuss, except with people like you who are vaguely on the same wavelength, though the results of our work are very different.

Muriel Spark when asked, "How do you write a novel?" replied: "I write down the title, and underneath that I write 'A Novel by Muriel Spark'. Then I put 'Chapter One' and I start writing."

When she says that, she's hiding from her questioner or from herself a subconscious process she would prefer not to understand.

If that's so she, like Beckett, should refuse to be interviewed. Beckett says: "I don't know how I write. I have nothing to add to what I've written. If I had I'd have written it." He won't talk about his work. He's about the only writer in the world who won't, so far as I know.

Except that so much of his work is writing about writing.

James Hanley, like many others, says, "Once I get to Chapter Three, the characters take over." I couldn't write like that. I always know what a novel's going to be about, I know its structure well beforehand. If I ever dry up, if there's ever no longer three novels in my head, perhaps I'll sit down and write, "So-and-so, a novel by B.S. Johnson," and off I'll go.

Meanwhile you have your trilogy in hand. How's it going? Will it be your best work yet?

I don't think of my books competing with each other. I haven't got a "best book" or anything like it. I very rarely go back and read my own work. In moments of despair, and there are lots of those, I will pick up a book to see how I did something in the past, or to confirm that I have written some books worth writing.

Tom Mallin

Tom Mallin was born on 14 June 1927 in West Bromwich. His father died when he was four, and he was charitably educated at a boarding school, and later went to the Birmingham School of Art, from where he won a scholarship to the Royal Academy. His art studies were interrupted when he was drafted into the army and between 1945 and 1947 he served much of his National Service in the Middle East. He moved to London and in 1949 married the American-born painter Muriel George. He trained as a picture restorer, while continuing to paint in his spare time and also contributing illustrations and cartoons to periodicals such as *Lilliput* and *Picture Post.* In 1955 Mallin moved to Suffolk with his wife and two sons, where he continued to work as a sculptor, painter and restorer until 1966 when he suffered a crisis of confidence in the visual arts. He buried most of his sculpture and destroyed many of his paintings and turned his attention to writing. When his first novel, *Dodecahedron* (1970), was published, Francis King wrote in the *Sunday Telegraph* that "it is amazing that a writer so gifted should only now be publishing his first novel at the age of 43". In the same year his first stage play, *Curtains,* was produced at the Tower Theatre in London, from where it went to the Edinburgh Festival under the direction of Michael Rudman at the Traverse Theatre. Mallin's other published novels are *Knut* (1971), *Erowina* (1972), *Lobe* (1977) and *Bedrok* (which was posthumously published in 1978). Mallin died of cancer on 21 December 1977. In the fifteen years before his death he produced over forty full-length novels and plays.

Mallin's intense, fast, joyful way of working was in direct contrast with the usual cliché of the artist suffering to produce a few sentences each day. Similarly, his willingness to reinvent whole countries he had never seen is at odds with the realistic novelist's research and information gathering.

MALLIN: My first published book was *Dodecahedron,* which was written in 1969 but came out in 1970, then *Knut,* then *Erowina,* written in 1965. They were published in the wrong order, like Shaw's books were published in the wrong order and they said he was getting better and better!
BURNS: *I thought your first novel was* Dodecahedron *and it struck me as an absolutely extraordinary first novel, but it was your third?*

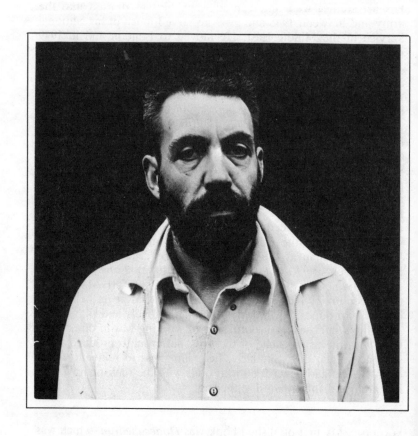

I'll tell you about that. There's also all the others I've destroyed, anyway not published, and there's one which keeps on being returned, I don't understand why, called *Fripp,* finished in '69. A lot were finished in 1969.

I've written two, four six, eight, eleven novels altogether but I wouldn't be seen dead with them apart from the last four, and I like *Fripp.*

Tell us a little about those unpublished books.

The first book was about *partisans!* Don't ask me why! I followed it with a book called *Dagbad,* then one about the seven deadly sins but linked. . . . The idea was that in this Middle East country a revolution was taking place, and there was this American who obviously was threatened because he was an American, and he took refuge with a money-lender (that was Greed). The money-lender tells him tales before he's moved on (he's trying to make his escape) and he's passed on to others, shopkeepers . . . and each abstracts something from him, rings, anything, and in the end he's . . . murdered. At the last he's in a tomb where he meets a man who's been there for ages and who lives on the snails who inhabit the tomb. Meant to be a fantasy fairy tale. That was written in the 'fifties, when I was painting, earning a living as a restorer. Then I gave up everything, in terms of regular non-writing employment. Now, instead of writing only in the evenings, I write from six in the morning until late at night, the whole day, non-stop.

When you were painting, restoring and writing, wasn't it exhausting?

When I work I'm totally submerged, I throw myself into everything. If I were collecting fish I'd go absolutely berserk about collecting fish. Anything I do I get totally absorbed in, and that's it. So fatigue didn't come into it. At the start I wrote all those books out in longhand. Then my wife said, "You ought to do something about all this," and I thought, I can't send away things in longhand so I bought a typewriter. As soon as I bought a typewriter I could no longer write in longhand. It was the cheapest portable and it broke. I got another cheap portable and that broke too. They all break, I wear them out. When I'm doing the final type I do it carefully, two fingers only, but when I'm composing I write so rapidly, I want to get it down so quickly, I use three or four or more fingers, to get it down before the idea disappears. If someone taps on the door and I'm halfway through a thought, it's gone, it's finished, I've had it! So initially I write *fast*, then when I've got it all down for the day or the week or whatever it is, then I have to say, come on, sort all this mess out and have a very careful look and see what you've got, you know, because your heart goes so fast! Calm down, and let's have a look at what you're doing! And try to make it readable and . . . work as a craftsman, I suppose.

You enjoy both jobs, the composing and the editing?

Oh, I enjoy it all. As soon as I sit down, I'm away! I adore it.

At that first meeting between you and the material, you must get it down fast?

I can tell you about that. I'm not one of those people, and there are some, who think ahead before they begin to type. They have firm ideas about what they would really like to write about. It's not like that for me. *Dodecahedron* happened very simply, from a curious set of coincidences. My wife had been watching Kenneth Clark's talks on Civilization and she came in and asked, "What is a dodecahedron?" I wrote it down, got my big dictionary, and kept saying, Dodeca, Dodeca, funny, that's a girl's name, then found it: twelve-sided figure. It was Easter, and I thought, Easter, twelve stations of the cross, and don't ask me what made me think of this jump: twelve-sided figure, twelve stations of the cross, Easter, Christ, and another thing which, I don't know, might bear on it, my eldest son brought back a film script by Bergman because at that time I was interested in writing film scripts, so *Dodecahedron* was written as a film script initially, and twelve . . . and twelve . . . it all came together, and I sat down and typed it, literally, which I'd never done before, in two weeks, simple as that. And yes, I was reading *The Lost Books of Eden,* parts of the Bible which have been banned, withdrawn from the Bible, and, at the beginning of *Dodecahedron* there are a number of quotes from this *Lost Book of Eden* . . . it tells how Jesus did *dead* little boys round a fish pool because they broke his clay duck, he deaded them! [*laughs*] which in a Bible you can't have, if it's Jesus, you see? And all this talk of his brothers and sisters, fascinating reading. All these things, all disparate, coincided, which somehow made me spring off into the tale. And because it's *Dodeca* and *hedron* I immediately thought of her not as Christ but going through these twelve terrible experiences. So that's the trigger. . . .

I wonder, particularly as Dodecahedron *was written as a film script (but not confined to a film script), is it, as you sit typing fast, as if you were watching a film and describing what you can see?*

I've been a painter, English painters tend to be literal, and I was literal. I don't think I was a very good painter but I was literal. This always worried me. I was certainly very talented, but being literal I saw images, all the time, I still do, very real images which I can walk into and inhabit, so if an image comes up, of a room, building, landscape, I *know* it, so well, immediately, that I can go *in* to it.

You said, when a building "comes up"?

It just appears. Say, "an old building". There are various words you might use to establish what sort of a place or landscape it's going to be, or a person: they assemble themselves visually, there they are, very real. With *Erowina* I'd been reading an American detective story, in which for the first time one was taken into a morgue and the body dissected, right? And I thought, that doesn't go far enough, so I started to write *Erowina*. It opens in a morgue, and Erowina is described from the crown of her head to her toes, and the more I travelled down this body, describing it and whatnot, the more clearly I saw this woman and how she had killed herself with a hat pin. I'd not worked out the rest of the story, I was just doing this . . . and there she was and I was intrigued to know more about her. I thought, having described the body, why not describe where she lives, *everything* about her? In fact the book was cut by half because it would have been massive – but nowhere in that massive book is there a description of Erowina, except when she's lying in the morgue. I don't think there's a description of anybody (unless memory betrays me). I also tried to get away from that "He said", "She replied", though in other books I haven't.

You avoid it in Dodecahedron.

That's because it started as a film script, then I took out the shots and locations and fiddled it like that – yes, fiddled, fiddled, reconstructed it. Whereas *Knut* was initially a film script called *Das Lust Haus,* which was the nearest I could get to Gazeba (lust house). I liked the film script so much and everybody kept turning it down – so I thought, dammit, I'd write it as a book, but by that time I was more interested in a minor character, a little boy who died, so I kept him alive and he became central to it.

The woman on the slab, in the morgue, Erowina, you say you described her, you could see her, so the question is: where did she come from? The possible simple answer to that is, Oh, well, she's my Auntie Tillie. But presumably it's not that simple, not simply someone you know?

When I think of where people come from, characters, situations, anything – I think of the clarity with which they appear in the first few words you use – you have a vague notion of what they are like, but with the first few words you use to describe them, you, as it were, start to clothe them, set them off. . . . I think a creative person is a person who switches so rapidly – if he

jumps from thought to thought he will then bring them together.
There are random things happening all the time and he brings
them together, and the bringing together sometimes gives you
such a clear image that it is very, very real.

Would you try and show how that process worked with
Erowina, *in more detail?*

Let's say I wanted to write about this body in the morgue. I set
out roughly what the analysis from head to toe would be. Then I
thought, this is not detailed enough, if this is going to be the only
description of her in the book I thought I wanted it in absolutely
meticulous detail.

*So people are either going to miss the whole point or get this into
their heads, to last the book through, rather than in Chapter Three
say she has a birthmark, and Chapter Six she had long hair? This
will last the long book through?*

Exactly. So having described her roughly as she lay on the slab,
I went back and described her in more detail. As soon as I more
or less got the shape, the female shape lying there, with the
various things that have happened to her, I went back and
described her minutely, and she suddenly – like Frankenstein's
monster – she suddenly got up off the table! There she was!
Absolutely real.

She appeared.

Absolutely.

*You still haven't quite answered the question: "Where did she
come from?"*

I wanted a woman who was about thirty to thirty-five. I got to
think about her, a woman of thirty-five who had probably not
really looked after herself all that well. How much fat will she
have on her? So, when you start taking measurements of fat, you
take your calipers and you divide by two right? Because you have
two thicknesses. So I pinched myself and had a look, and I
thought, a woman would be a bit fattier here, and I looked up my
anatomical books and whatnot.

Did you?

Well, I studied anatomy, you see. And that was one point
where I knew that I'd got it. I can't describe it in terms, as to say,
"As far as here" or "Down to her knees" but at some point she
certainly became very real.

*This is at the beginning of the book. Did you at that stage
envisage the context in which she would live, which would give her
certain characteristics?*

I had no idea. When I decided that she'd committed suicide
with a pin – you must remember I was writing a detective story,

this was not a very original way of murder or whatever – I thought it would be self-inflicted but I had no idea why. I just wanted this body in the morgue on the slab, and it was only later I made her pregnant, about a year later, it took a long time, about a year later I made her pregnant and put that in.

A conventional novelist's way of creating a character is to take a bit of someone they've known, a bit of someone seen in the street, all that stuff. Do you work like that at all?

Very rarely. In fact *Fripp* is the only slightly autobiographical book I've ever written, yet it isn't.

Well, there are bits and scraps of you, there's the man with the iron-grey hair — does it surprise you to hear that?

You mean as Hedron? No, never occurred to me. I can describe him, I can see him, but it's not like looking in the mirror, I never thought of myself. . . .

But, just as we say that people's pet dogs look like their owners because instinctively they choose themselves, but unaware, do you, as it were, choose. . . .

Ah, well, you see, I write fiction. Now to me this is all imagination, as far as I'm concerned. There are people who when they write fiction have to have the right aeroplane flights, the right times for the trains. I dislike this intensely. I know there are people who do it and have great fun with it, but I dislike it. All my books, except for *Erowina* which is set in a part of London I know, they're all set in places I've never been to, Sweden, Middle East, and *Lobe*, a very strange book, is set in Yugoslavia. Therefore I can create from imagination, I don't want to be accurate as regards that. But coming back to *Erowina*, you're dead right, I did *describe* in one chapter, where they have a meal in a Greek restaurant and go on to a club afterwards, and they are all real people.

But that's the exception?

That was the exception, that was deliberate because at that time a writer who shall be nameless had written a book about my friend, and my friend and I couldn't find his character in the book. In other words we were seeing differently, and I thought I'd do an accurate assessment in a description, but so far no one seems to have recognized themselves and it's the only time I've ever done it. What initiated me was that someone, having been told they'd been written about, couldn't recognize themselves in the book and I couldn't recognize them either. So, as it were in reply, I wrote what I thought was accurate. I don't know if they read the book or not but so far I've had no come-backs.

I see two elements working together: the characters you draw have no source in your friends or family. And there is the deliberate projection into a land that you've never been in. The result is an attempt to abstract *the whole fictional process? To remove fiction from social reality? You attempt to disconnect the scene you describe from social reality, and as far as you can, to disconnect it from yourself, which creates a very clinical, clear, almost scientific style?*

I would have thought it was a more imaginative style because if I was going to set it in a real place I'd have all this bother of making the buses run to time, and really it's so boring. . . .

Of course it is. When I say your style is precise and scientific I don't mean that in contrast to imaginative work or in any way incompatible with that. On the contrary. Take Kafka, The Trial *or* The Castle *which are clearly set not in a "real" country but in an imagined land. Yet as part of the skill that creates that we get Kafka's meticulous, incomparable eye for physical detail. That's what I mean by work which combines scientific precision, a marvellously observant eye, plus an attempt to disconnect the novel from a known scene. And you're in that line, that territory?*

I agree with that. It is deliberate.

Further: if you site a novel in a place you know, in a sense your imagination can relax. You can write "Oxford Street" and you've no need to describe the particular characteristics of Oxford Street, the label is enough. The lazy writer and the lazy reader collaborate and the result is stodge, unimaginative stodge. Whereas you compel yourself and you compel your reader to follow you, into a territory in which, starting from scratch, you've got to describe everything, because that which you don't describe will not exist?

Yes. You must also understand that I write plays as well as novels. A play does exist in front of people's eyes. Therefore, if you like, in compensation for the "unreality" of the novels I have the "reality" of the plays using those words in a special, limited sense.

Just as Kafka wrote Amerika *not having been, so you create countries, people, "from your imagination". But the ultimate source of all the contents of your imagination is social reality? As Miro said, "To leap in the air, you must start with your feet on the ground." That's true too, isn't it?*

Yes.

So there's a certain gap in your description of your writing process. We get this highly-wrought meticulously observed "reality", and then there's everyday life. What is the connection between the two?

If you said to me now: Draw me a street or a person, I'd do it, but I'd ask you for just one or two more details. Is it an English country town or is it an English city? Is it abroad? Is the person with high cheek-bones coming from the East? Just one or two little points. Then I'll sit down and draw you in great detail with loving care, the person or the place. I'll do that! To me it's the same as writing about it. Once I've got one or two points I can start to wonder, and think how she sits. . . . And then she'll take over, or the town, or the view.

One of your particular talents, therefore, is to take off from a generalization or hardly more, into the particular. You illustrated that when talking of Erowina: "Well, she's about thirty-five." Now that's a thoroughly unremarkable thing to say of a woman. But you went straight from that to a stunning sentence: "How much fat will she have on her?" That, for me, is a perfect example of how to travel straight, fast and true from the general to the particular.

When I make that jump I find I immediately have hundreds of other jumps going on, that's why I have initially to work fast. I don't want to lose them. I can't write them down in longhand fast enough, so I have to get to the typewriter and get as much down as I possibly can, and suddenly she or he stands up, large, and illumined. Then I'm happy. Once I've got them, then they can start to do things "on their own", though they've still got to walk in rooms and across landscapes I create for them. You might go into a shop every day to buy cigarettes and only see the shop-keeper from the waist up, he's somehow part of the shelves, he's there. But when you meet him in the street you don't recognize him! The background's different! He's got legs! So you have to build the background for them, but they themselves *have* a background.

Once they have been made, then they'll begin to make things?

They'll begin to move and relate. It can be very difficult when characters you've given a few words to say will say things that surprise you, things you never dreamt they'd say.

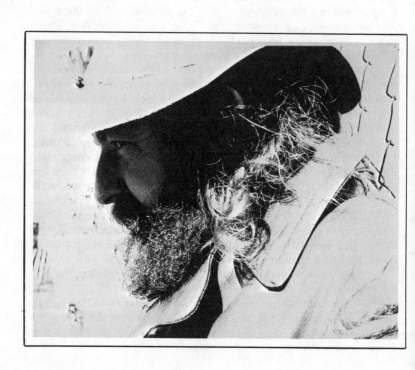

Michael Moorcock

Michael Moorcock was born in Surrey in 1939. He has been a singer-guitarist, a farm worker and editor of a boys' magazine called *Tarzan Adventures*. For seven years (1964–71), he was editor and publisher of *New Worlds*, an outstanding science-fiction magazine, and he has edited numerous collections of science fiction. He is a successful and prolific author (having written over fifty books) whose work includes science fiction but extends to other genres. His many novels include the Jerry Cornelius tetralogy, *The Final Programme* (1968), *A Cure for Cancer* (1971), *The English Assassin* (1972) and *The Condition of Muzak* (winner of the Guardian Fiction Prize, 1977); *Behold the Man* (1968), *The Bull and the Spear* (1973), *The Oak and the Ram* (1973), *The Sword and the Stallion* (1974), *Breakfast in the Ruins* (1972), *Gloriana* (1978), and *Byzantium Endures* (1981).

Moorcock has the reputation of being avant-garde while still remaining popular and commercially successful — this is obviously a considerable feat. His popular Jerry Cornelius has been featured on film. He wrote political pamphlets for the Liberal Party in the early sixties and later wrote for the underground press. His work is often concerned with the effects of imperialism, and he says that even his fantasy novels "deal with moral problems rather than magical ones."

MOORCOCK: Recently a New York college held a summer school in London and they got me along to answer questions about my work. They were doing Creative Writing in the States. It was very good money for me, but a dreadful ordeal, more like a show trial than anything. These very intelligent kids tore my books to pieces. I was soon saying: "You're right! You're right! I recant!" The SF fans had read all my science fiction and didn't like the rest. They insisted on talking about SF which I consider to be very minor and I can't remember it anyway. No sweat went into it so I have no recollection of what I did.

BURNS: *The afficionados knew your work better than you did?*

Absolutely. Then there were the people who were out to get me. Out to get anybody. Because they were far brighter than me. And they knew it. They were so much more confident. I don't want to be too paranoid about it. They didn't understand the emotional investment I have in the work. They picked up a lot of little self-indulgences I put into *The Final Programme*. Little facts. Things that weren't true. I had Jerry Cornelius playing a guitar with six pick-ups. You don't need six pick-ups on a guitar. In fact I'd done it for extra-indulgence, for waste, because the whole book was about waste. Of course the kids hadn't caught on to that, so I tried to explain it in their terms, saying, well, he could have had six amps, each one picking up . . . finally I just said, "It's true, I confess, I am an enemy of the state!"

What would you have preferred to talk about?

Practical technique: How I go about organizing material. What I put in and what I leave out. How I structure a specific kind of book. How I structure it, first if it's one kind of book, how I develop the structure as I go along if it's another kind of book. The difference between writing a social novel and writing an imaginative novel or whatever it's called. The trouble is there's no appropriate vocabulary. The lack of a vocabulary makes most critics unable to review your books and mine, certainly those of my books I'd like to be seriously reviewed. Jimmy Ballard's another writer who gets reviewed in funny terms because the critics are unfamiliar with the technique employed, and are floundering with their vocabulary. If a critic's reading eight bad social novels that week, and then gets one of mine or yours, they need to switch —

Your work should be in a different category?

Yes, with a different kind of critic reading it. It might well be mere literary extremism, which will shift back into and reinvigorate the traditional novel. But we need to talk of "movements" in order to get moving, to get any kind of dynamic. We need to think, "We're eight blokes here, eight musketeers."

But it isn't like that, is it?

Yes, finally it comes down to individual writers. Movements always break up very fast. The *New Worlds* group soon broke up (quite amicably) into individual writers, each getting on with his own work, some doing quite traditional stuff, whereas before they'd been trying to experiment. . . . Each feeling secretly that the rest really don't know what they're doing, which was another part of it.

The religious element?

Or the self-delusion element, it comes to the same thing: the need to dismiss everything that's been done up to three months ago as so much shit. Poetry movements tend to do this: wild claims, throwing everything out. Traditional critics say you're throwing out the baby with the bathwater, and that's what you are doing, that's the whole point, you want to get rid of the baby too. Until you reach a point where you're easy with what you've got, you can look back on it, you're more tolerant, you can even bring bits of the baby back in. You need to lie to yourself for a short time but it's not necessary to stick to the colours you nailed up in 1929, when you and eight other blokes "formed the Movement". Just as the Surrealist movement disclaimed some of its most interesting members because they didn't stick to the Manifestos.

With *New Worlds,* after the first flush, I could predict when certain people would move away from each other. I could anticipate to some extent when rows would erupt in order to create this (necessary) split. Or when new authors would assert their independence from the magazine which had originally provided their stimulus, and reject it.

In addition to editing New Worlds *you wrote for it?*

I liked doing serials in *New Worlds:* it's based on a love of magazines, the immediacy of magazines. I enjoyed having to do fifteen thousand words a month, or whatever, to supply it, control it, with all the discipline involved in trying to do a good piece of work in a relatively short time.

Is the stuff you do for magazines as good as the stuff in thick covers?

It's often the same stuff. I did *A Cure for Cancer* as a serial and it's the most mandarin thing I've ever written, it's too pretentious and obscure, too many private jokes, everything I dislike in someone like Nabokov. The funny thing is that though it's packed with references it was written very fast, to deadlines.

When you work at speed do you not have to dig up images and ideas? Are they there on the surface?

Completely the opposite. *Cure for Cancer* took three years before it got written. Say ten thousand words of it, and bits and notes took a good three years, probably more, and perhaps five years between conception and publication. *The English Assassin* took about three years, too.

What happens during that time?

Thinking about it, structuring it, gathering material, sifting material. Then I write it fast. Each section of *The English Assassin* was written at a sort of white heat. Written suddenly, straight down. Exhaustion followed. Then the whole thing came together, was written and re-written. I put that book through three drafts. The beginning went through about eight, and suffers accordingly, it's much more stilted than the rest.

There's a lengthy incubation period before the "sudden" time, the coming together of all the scattered bits?

Yes, for a book of that kind.

During that time you are thinking about the book directly, focusing on it? Or do you work in a more receptive fashion, mooning around like a poet, waiting for it to steal up on you?

I think it's half-and-half. I dunno, a bit o' this and a bit o' that. . . . Sometimes I'll actually have a moment when the expression is clear, and the means of dealing with it. I know what I want to put in. Other times I just let it all come in and sort itself out.

When there comes into your mind a bit you can use or that relates to the job in hand, do you make a mental note or do you write it down?

I write it down. I note a piece of dialogue, or a character or an observation. I keep two notebooks: an open book and a locked book. The open book is for general notes and the locked book is for very specific observation of people I know. It's locked because I keep their real names in at that stage, I've got a very poor memory and I couldn't remember them otherwise. The book contains revelations about my friends, which I don't want them to see. And there's self-revelation which perhaps I don't want people to know about either. I'm not very secretive but there are certain things which might do me harm if people. . . . I keep two Twinlock files so the sheets can be transferred, if they get too hot, from the open to the locked book. Other people probably write in code or remember more closely, but I have to note it down fairly quickly if I want to remember a pointed observation. Obviously I don't use the stuff straight, or anything like it. But sometimes, as you know, you just pick up a sense of perhaps a relationship between a couple of people, or yourself and somebody, or whatever. It's stuff you wouldn't talk about, which you wouldn't want them to know because it might upset or even anger them, but which in the context of fiction ninety per cent of the time they wouldn't recognize. I keep the book locked simply because we have a lot of visitors and obviously some of them are going to . . . possibly come across it. It's not paranoid, just extra caution.

For example, a girl I know was telling me about her mother. All the girl's boyfriends are hippies, or her mother sees them as hippies, so her mother said the girl "didn't need to worry about getting pregnant off the hippies, but if you ever get a real man you'll find yourself up the stick in no time." Nothing much, but that is what she told me. She's working as a waitress and she tells me things about waitressing and the relationships between herself and the other waitresses and what goes on.

Did you make the note immediately you got home?

I did it the next morning. I see [*reads the entry*] I didn't use my usual pen I keep in my dressing-gown pocket.

You got the exact turn of phrase?

No. The girl and her mother aren't English, and I've translated it into Cockney language and Cockney situation, because it's the sort of thing Mrs Cornelius would say to her daughter Catherine. I was working out the sort of milieu Catherine could be living in and I began to see that she could be working in a café in Ladbroke Grove.

I tend not to make notes immediately. Usually I sleep on it and make notes first thing in the morning. Anything that doesn't survive the night is probably no good anyway. During the night I lie there thinking about things. Other things get added. If I'd made a note straight after talking with that girl I'd have written it straight, but by the morning there's an extra dimension added. It's Mrs Cornelius talking to Catherine, it's Catherine's job and Catherine's boyfriends.

It's such a grinding job that girl described, such low money for such long hours, in a sort of semi-sexy tourist place. The girls have to wear hot pants, which suits few of them, but they have to wear them because they're "sexy". They get a lot of out-of-town businessmen, they get a lot of abuse and very little in the way of tips. It isn't as if the money made it worth doing. It's the kind of job you get when you're fairly desperate. So it struck me that it was the kind of job Catherine would be doing.

There was an element of social criticism in it?

Yes, I don't believe anyone should have to put up with that to earn a living. It's dehumanizing. I think most work is, but this was worse than most.

Did you decide to describe the working conditions in your book to help change them? Do you think your book will tend to have that effect?

No, it will only provide a focus for people who are already fairly sensitive to that sort of situation – the way Angus Wilson's best observations work for me, saying things I've felt but haven't had the language to express.

I imagine you slotting in a lot of material like that. But are there things you can't use so easily? You know they'll come in handy but you don't know when?

I write so much, so fast, that that doesn't happen often. I work in so many different areas. A quasi-poetic image that occurs to me in one of my more purple moments can go into a fantasy. A piece of generalized philosophizing can also go into one of those fantasies because they have no specific social context. I'm doing so much. I write editorials, so if I get an idea about the current state of publishing or whatever, then that immediately goes into the non-fiction notebook for fairly immediate use. If I don't use that kind of note soon it never gets used.

Do you carry a notebook around with you?

Yes, but I rarely use it. If I do it's usually pointless because when I go out I'm mostly either stoned or playing with a band. Most of my goings-out are fairly frenetic — Hydian as opposed to Jeykellian. I usually like to go out and sit in a corner or in the back of a rock band's van and just be fairly stoned on my own.

Can you write in that state?

No, I've tried and it's useless. Occasionally I get the odd phrase but almost always I write nonsense. I get stoned completely outside my normal writing environment, in pubs, or at concerts, or with non-literary friends. It's almost like dreaming, it's an imaginative pleasure, there's very little verbal going on. I may be picking up the way Hell's Angels move around and consider themselves and what they do, what they say, but I'm not making notes, I'm just getting the emotional thing.

You're describing a process of oblique observation. Not looking straight at it, but out of the corner of your eye.

The things I do have to look straight at are the moral implications, and the way I organize my work. I have to face the moral implications however nasty they are, and however much they may clash with my superficial wish to make a point. If the morals don't fit I have to look at the work again and find out what it means to me. Every two or three years I shift into a new phase of work, a new area of exploration. And then I get very depressed and lonely and hard, and start looking at the work very hard, and attempt to resolve it in moral terms. At that stage I tend to produce a book which is too specific, a novel which is evidently doing certain things. *Breakfast in the Ruins* was a pure example of that. It's a badly fragmented book. The elements aren't meshed. That's the result of my first moral step, which produces a novel which is to some extent a blueprint, with ideas which reappear below the surface of the next, more subtle book. In *Breakfast in the Ruins* I've got children dying, social injustice, and corruption. Simple moral images. No ambiguities. The main character is corrupted and brutalized and in turn brutalizes and corrupts. There's also a certain homosexual element in it, a personal aspect, I'm looking at the potential homosexual aspect of myself, facing it, and facing other aspects of myself. The "What Would You Do?" sections of the book are personal notes, drawn from my own situation, accrued things, basic things, presented to myself to make me face them, make me push further, personally and morally, to force myself a little bit harder, and hopefully to bring more self-knowledge.

Breakfast in the Ruins, then, is the opening of a new phase of exploration of an evolving moral attitude, and because you're starting something new you tend to be unaware of the subtleties and to be too direct. You progress from the direct to the oblique. Having established the moral structure almost like a cartoon, in strong unequivocal lines, you can then become more tentative?

Right. So I can forget it too. I've made that decision and faced those facts and got through the depression, because as you know there's a lot of dreadful depression involved. Facing self-deception is the worst thing. Once I've done it, once I've made a moral act of writing a book that is self-revealing . . . I collapse. But I find I get two or three years of quite easy working after that.

Do the needs of the book ever clash with your moral pre-occupations?

I don't have an established moral view. I'm pretty amoral personally. I'm a kind of socialist because I think that's right, and emotionally it fits, but I'm not like that when I'm writing. It's the moral implications within the work. In the Jerry Cornelius books and in *Breakfast in the Ruins* I produced the structure first. I divided it up. I knew roughly what I was going to do in each section. So the structure was there, and if the moral development of the book clashed with that, I had to re-think the structure and its effect.

I began in what was almost an imagist school of science fiction, which depended very strongly on the image and to a degree on the symbol that the image represents. Not symbolism, but going in that direction. The kind of SF I like is Ballard's and the best of Aldiss. It has a very simple plot, perhaps like a Stevenson short story, where the plot will be barely important, and the images, the moods and atmosphere are the key thing. The images are usually romantic, some kind of nature imagery, though not always. Where the image will make or have moral reverberations you have to find the image that connects most closely with the moral feeling you have about the book, it's no more than a feeling. The act of writing, as you know, is one that brings out, clarifies the moral aspects of things. I write it more or less to find out. At one time I could explore ideas through "moral tales", either science fiction or fantasies. But probably the fantasies in their essential appeal are, to the socialist in me, morally reprehensible.

How do you get round that?

I generalize. I put generalized humane philosophizing into the fantasies, to oppose the images. The fantasies depend almost wholly on paradox, their appeal lies in paradox. I can put in an image that strikes me as a bit dicey but I balance it either with action or another image.

Even the nasty bits in your books are done in a life-enhancing way, they make me feel good. That's the effect of your energy, your "life-force" morality.

Fantasy writers like Lovecraft and others write out of an incredible neurotic, unhealthy, perverse inability to live. Most of them, in the 1930s, and the nineteenth-century Gothic writers too, tended to be reclusive, and a bit nasty in their attitudes. I can't face doing that. I produce the same kind of image as them but the context is lighter. The really heavy fantasy fans probably find my stuff too mild. It's like pornography: I don't produce "hard-core" fantasy. I'm just naturally healthy! Physically I'm healthy, that's a lot of it. You can rely on it too much but if you have a lot of energy, if you were a lusty healthy infant with few illnesses, it informs the way you look at things, and it gives you more energy to work. I find the more I write the more I enjoy writing and the better I write. The year I wrote ten books, two were among my best, and eight were fantasies. I done over thirty fantasies. I write them straight down, without pre-planning and without re-writing. I once said to Tom Disch that from one image he would write a poem while I'd write a fantasy. I deliberately use a much more diffuse framework than a poem. A fantasy and a poem are opposites in form, yet they may be essentially the same in content. A poet sits and writes a poem about a waterfall, whereas I'll use a waterfall as a central image in a fantasy. I did that in one book. I can't remember which, I can't remember any of them. I never read them except occasionally to check something, because they form one big unit, they intersect constantly, the characters move in and out, the cosmology has become extremely complicated, with dimensions and planes and spheres of existence and so on, and recurring names in different fantasies meaning different things.

You write these fantasies so fast: do you just tune in to your subconscious and then indulge in something like automatic writing?

A lot of my fans of the madder kind believe I may be in tune with something, but I know it comes largely from my childhood, out of the mind that was formed then. All the characters in a fantasy have to be childish or adolescent in order to function.

Because they're larger than life their emotions are huge, their ambitions and destinies vast. Many of the heroes are tragic heroes facing adolescence and the implications of adolescence. They meet general but nonetheless profound realities, often disguised as fantasies but closely related to sexual awakening. Like Elric's big black sword and his inability to understand its power and the power it has over him. I'm conscious of this while writing it, and have been pretty much from the start. It also means that cynically I can produce books that have the strongest possible appeal on the unconscious sexual plane.

That partly accounts for their popularity?

Yes, but they're not written cynically, they're not written to exploit. I put a lot into them. I hope I don't give the reader a bad read, but I can conceive what he wants and give it to him. The genre is quite large now, and with the exception of Fritz Leiber (a very good humorous fantasy writer) I'm about the only person writing the stuff knowingly and countering the unhealthy aspects. Morally I couldn't write them unless I did. In all fantasies there's a tendency towards fascism, towards thinking in terms of social pyramids, basic fascistic ideas and images. I write about heroes, so I contradict that by leading always to final statements where gods and heroes and grand designs are shown to be pointless. It's reasonable: I give people a good read but I don't let them go off with the wrong ideas!

Your fantasies read to me a bit like dreams. Do you put your dreams into them?

If I have a good one. I dream very prosaically. They're usually very ordinary, unpleasant situations. If they're nightmares it's something very likely to happen, like my wife with some bloke I can't stand. My dreams are sometimes extremely strong, revealing whole areas of desire which I've no conception of normally, things I could do in certain circumstances . . . I had an incredibly intense homosexual dream in which I was completely passive, giving in to a very powerful and real person. I've always pushed my fantasies as far as they would go. I obviously can't experience everything to the limit, there isn't the time or energy. But occasionally I have a revelation that does make me re-assess things: where I thought I had pushed myself to a certain limit, and I had, but *away* from the real thing. . . .

So what seemed self-expression was really self-repression?

Right. A slight advance possibly. I think I'm on to something and I'm congratulating myself that I've hung on to it, I'm doing my job . . . then I have a dream that just blows it. It happens two or three times a year. It's me saying to myself, come off it, that isn't what you're supposed to be doing, a sort of knuckle-rapping dream. I usually write the dream down, but that definitely goes into the locked notebook! Very hard to take but you just have to take it. Essential experience for a writer. That's my aesthetic view of writing, my puritanical Leavisite view. I admire Leavis's moral fervour, his emotionalism. I don't always agree with him but he's got such dedication, such force, such a will to attack that I always find him stimulating even though he's often lying to himself. And George Orwell's essays are superb for *that,* for hanging on, getting his teeth in, not caring whom he offends. But he's also lying to himself finally . . . because only fiction can tell the truth! You can't tell the truth in non-fiction, it's not a suitable form! You always have to talk yourself into a line of argument to produce a nice essay. But I enjoy good clearly written essays of the Orwell kind, and Stevenson. I can't abide people like George Steiner, basically because he's too stupid. I don't like the synthetic sort of essay Steiner writes in which he'll be into a lot of things he doesn't know much about and will dazzle the reader for a while. But underneath there's basically a few very stupid ideas.

Where did you learn to appreciate that stuff?

Not at school. I left school at fifteen and they taught me nothing, except touch-typing. My education was a complete waste of time apart from a couple of years at a Rudolph Steiner school, a very humane system of education which tried to encourage the child's imagination, with heavy emphasis on acting, painting and dance. Rudolph Steiner's mystical Christianity, and his ability to conceive a complex supernatural cosmology, came in very useful for my fantasies.

As a "neurotic child of a broken home", with an extremely highly-strung mother, I developed a rich fantasy life which possibly dominated the rest of my life. When I was fifteen I had a lot of bad working experiences which I hope never to repeat. Then I got a job as an office boy in a firm of management consultants. They were very kind. They saw me as some sort of boy wonder. Presumably I was very imaginative and they didn't normally get office boys like me. My main job was to go to the library for the boss twice a week to pick up a book for him and "one for myself". I was very lucky. That was the best situation I had. It gave me experience of different areas of society. Some were engineers and I learnt from them. Some were very posh so I went with them to posh places. They were incredibly good to me. I hardly worked at all, it was just like play school. They lent me the office duplicator to print all the magazines I used to do. I think I just appealed to their imaginations. So there was that.

And low-life Soho which I got into very early. I don't think I was
escaping from society, though I thought I was at the time.

You were almost escaping into *it?*

I still do. I haven't changed much. My whole imaginative area
is dirty cellars, three o'clock in the morning, looking for a dog-
end. I read Henry Miller and, later, Kerouac, that whole seedy
romanticism, or romantic seedyism, which leads to Burroughs. It
was the attraction of contemporary bohemianism. And the
writing thing, I got early into that. I wrote my first fantasy series
when I was sixteen, and I suppose my first novel, *The Final
Programme,* in 1965 when I was twenty-five. And I played the
guitar. Mainly Soho. Mainly solo. I'm self-taught. My big regret
is that I've little musical theory and so haven't developed as
far as I'd like. But I play the guitar, alone or with bands, and
make records. . . .

*From what you've said I think maybe your music is spontaneous
and "unread", but your writing is heavily structured?*

Superficially I work on very clear structures. I find I can divide
a book into a beginning section, normally two middle sections,
and a concluding section. Which might not be apparent. Introduction, Development, Conclusion, is basically how I work on
everything.

Introduction is laying the ground for the whole thing. It's free-
wheeling enough, anyway it's the first bit I write. Then the
Development: usually the first section of the Development arises
from what's gone before, in the Introduction. But the second
section of the Development projects forward, it pre-figures the
Conclusion: I get to know my characters, develop their lives, going
back in time from the Introduction, I flesh it out. The second
section of the Development deals with how it's all going to end,
so I start seeding in elements which will emerge in the Conclusion.

I do a superstructure, almost in code form. Say I'm trying to
formulate the material, get it in some sort of shape, I'll write
down: "Development". In some of the Jerry Cornelius short
stories, which were all said to be formless, I've actually got those
words into the stories: "Introduction", "Development",
"Conclusion". And the stories fall into those sections. In all the
Cornelius books I use the central image of entropy throughout,
of disintegration of personal relationships and society, which I
see as permanently disintegrating. So the scientific concept of
entropy as an inevitable force runs through all my books. And
the simple moral in all of them is love conquers all.

*That's good to know. But does conquering mean defeating the
disintegrating process?*

No, it's going on. . . . It's peace and love really, basic hippy philosophy . . . if two people can love each other they create the foundation on which this perpetual process of disintegration can be overcome, or stalled.

Doesn't your view of society in disintegration, like a collapsing star, force you to adopt a consistently disintegrating form, with the paragraphs and sentences themselves fragmented in the Burroughs fashion?

A Cure for Cancer was deliberately fragmented in the way you describe. And the Conclusion of the book is pretty much at the centre, while the Development sort of falls away from it: a very complicated structure!

Even A Cure for Cancer *plays about with form in a way that only demonstrates the need for form.*

I couldn't write a formless novel, though a lot of my stuff is said to be formless by many people, a big mélange of jolly fun. But in fact it's very much the opposite. Maybe I do depend too much on form. I have a natural ability to structure my work, and as an editor I can teach it to others too. It's something I can do. But it can become a weakness. Perhaps I've got to go further, out of form. Being lazy, or scared, I fall back on form.

In writing a traditional, social novel, the subject matter dictates what you're going to do, the characters are so important they set off the whole development of the book. The attraction of that is partly why I seem to be retreating (if that's the right word) back towards the social novel. *Behold the Man* was closer to the social novel than my early SF, and *Breakfast in the Ruins* was closer still. The last Jerry Cornelius novel not only deals with certain moral imperfections in the first three books but is also much more of a social novel. My interest in individual character and in people grows as I live longer, so I grow towards the social novel as the only way to cope with the specific things I've got to write. Though it's much harder for me to write a social novel than to do the other.

Isn't that an indication that you should do the other?

No, because there are certain things I want to express through the techniques I've been developing over the last, say, five years. I've learned a lot, partly by writing and partly by "copying" classics. My novel *The Ice Schooner* was a copy of *The Rescue* by Conrad. I copied the basic moral situation and the basic relationships between the characters. I made a new book, the original wouldn't be recognizable, but I did it to see and experience how it was done. I've also learned from Angus Wilson, who to my mind is the best social novelist we've got (which might sound odd written down but I don't mean it that way). He is an extremely good, fine-pointed observer of human follies and human nobility as well. He captures specific kinds of people in particular situations which strike me as being very very likely and very truthful and it's something that I'd like to do a little more. In *The English Assassin* it's already there. A little more in sequence, a little more nuance of character.

Is that why it was rather well received? It's as if with that book you turned the corner towards acceptance. You know that dismissive kind of criticism? The English Assassin *wasn't treated like that.*

Sure. It's a more serious novel, it's deeper. But it's been noticed less than my previous books which got a lot of publicity. But the reviews were more serious, perhaps partly due to the jacket which was more restrained. With *The Final Programme* every critic described it as a comic-strip novel because it had a comic strip on the jacket. Practically every review of that book was a review of the jacket. In fact *The English Assassin* plays on the harsher aspects of life, but I don't think anybody saw what I was getting at, because I did it in a comic, elliptical way. It was a much sadder book than my previous work.

How much does the reception of one book influence the style of the next?

Obviously you have to go your own way and I've gone out on a limb with *The English Assassin* and with *Breakfast in the Ruins*. But I was writing about things I thought the majority of my audience had experienced. I wasn't writing for the critics, though the critics do represent the audience more than we'd like to admit, though readers tend to be more generous than critics. I now want to write in a more accessible style, but the funny thing is that someone I know who is almost illiterate liked *A Cure for Cancer* much more than *The English Assassin*, though the former is a far more literary book. You can't tell how it will affect people, but a book's reception is very important to me. I want as large an audience as possible. I don't write with any specific type of reader in mind, only friends, who aren't typical. When I'm writing something that I know a certain friend will like, I think, oh, he'll like this, he'll enjoy this bit.

Do you show early drafts to anyone?

All the time. I've no confidence. Especially to my wife, she's a very good critic, not a sympathetic one. I show the work to people I can trust to a degree (you can't really trust your friends, obviously), friends who will point out things they don't like, or say if something hasn't come off. They only echo what I really suspect and wish wasn't true. I know I've got to rewrite it but I don't want to, and I think if a friend says he likes it I may not have to, but he never does.

Can you help others the way others help you?

Yes. It's the editorial impulse which I've always had very strongly. On occasions I've deliberately restrained my own contributions to *New Worlds* in order to make a bridge between my work (which readers were familiar with) and the work of a writer I admire strongly. I don't do it much now but I used to. I did it with Burroughs in the late 'fifties when Burroughs was getting no attention at all. I put stuff in the magazine which would gradually help people understand Burroughs. A lot of stuff I wrote for *New Worlds* in the early days of editing it was done in this way.

My experience of magazine-editing showed that whenever we made an innovation readers screamed until they got used to it. My whole editorial plan for *New Worlds* was gradually to familiarize readers with what I regarded as the best current fiction. We did that with reviews as well. We created a readership – I don't think I'm being too egocentric – at least we helped it to emerge a little earlier than it otherwise would. We opened up the whole thing, in the States and here. It was *New Worlds* that did it. We completely widened the spectrum. We made it possible for any writer who wrote in that style to get published. We published far too many, because you don't get many good writers coming along. Us, and to some extent Judy Merril, an American lady anthologist in the mid 1960s: she was inspired by *New Worlds*. She was the first American prophet!

What are you writing now?

I usually have about a year's work in hand. I've got four more books to do this year (I'm slipping, I was doing one a month). They're all sorts, one's comic, one's a fantasy. . . . You see, it's all contracted for, so many books for one publisher, so many for another.

I'd like to be able to write two or three extremely good conventional novels about specific characters. Clive Allison suggested I write a three-decker set in late-Victorian and Edwardian society, which I'd quite like to do, as I'm familiar with the period. But there's a lot of people writing pastiche novels at the moment and I'm not sure I want to add to it. The novel is going through a bad phase, all novels are genre novels, particularly Margaret Drabble's. By genre novels I mean social novels. They're like detective novels now, there's no difference. They follow an absolutely prescribed course. They're unconscious genre fiction, and they're reviewed in genre terms. It's just another genre. It's descended to that. In such a situation I wonder if it's worth conceiving another pastiche. People who find it impossible to do something *fresh*, like John Fowles, say, or John Barth, they return, in Barth's case to the seventeenth-century picaresque, and in Fowles's case to *The French Lieutenant's Woman*. To my sure knowledge there's five or six books of the kind written, being written, or about to be published. *The French Lieutenant's Woman* is completely wrong, it just doesn't work, in spite of the "careful research". Good stuff's instinctive. I don't research anything, I just read in the period, magazines etc., and I've got all kinds of ephemera. But I'm not sure if I want to do it. I might scrap it. Which would be a pity. I could probably do it better than anyone.

Grace Paley

Grace Paley was born in New York City in 1922 to Mary Ridnyik Goodside and Isaac Goodside, a doctor whom she describes as "M.D., artist, and storyteller". She studied at Hunter College and at New York University. In 1942 she married Jess Paley, a movie cameraman, and they had two children. She is now married to a second husband, Robert Nichols, a poet and play-wright. After teaching at Columbia University and Syracuse University in the early 'sixties, she joined the faculty of Sarah Lawrence College, where she teaches in the Department of Literature and Writing.

Although she apparently thought of being a writer from an early age, Grace Paley's first collection of stories, *The Little Disturbances of Man*, did not appear until 1959. In 1961, she was awarded a Guggenheim fellowship in fiction, and throughout the 1960s she published stories in such magazines as *Atlantic*, *New American Review* and *Esquire*. Her first publisher allowed *The Little Disturbances of Man* to go out of print about 1965, but it was reissued in hardcover by Viking Press in 1968, was well received and appeared in paperback. Her second collection, *Enormous Changes at the Last Minute*, appeared in 1974.

Because her subject-matter could be called "domestic" and her stories often centre on "feisty" women, the feminist movement has brought Grace Paley increased attention. But Tillie Olsen, another superb woman writer, has warned that whenever writers are put in a special category, whether it be "women's writer", "proletarian writer", or "black writer", their work is being subtly devalued, someone is putting them on a reservation. It's impor-tant, then, not to overdomesticate Paley's work (not to worry – she'd never let 'em get away with it). She writes often of family life, of children, of "love", of friendship between women. These are tremendously important subjects in themselves, but, as her answers to questions printed here show, she knows that these subjects are related to history, that having a stake in one means having a stake in the other. The European holocaust is still having consequences in hundreds of thousands of families; nuclear power plants are affecting the reproductive tissue that makes families possible. These are some of the reasons why one of Paley's characters refers to the "cruel history of Europe" as "one of my known themes", while another concludes by saying that "directed out of that sexy playground by my children's heartfelt brains, I thought more and more every day about the world".

These are also some of the reasons why Paley, who once said that her politics were "anarchist, if that's politics", has been active with the War Resisters League and other groups. It's why she has been in jail and is willing to go back again, to stop the murdering of the young. She was very involved in the movement to end the Vietnam war, and in 1979 was arrested on the White House lawn in a demonstration against nuclear weapons. Politics in our century has been a grim business, and going to jail sounds grim, but there is nothing grim about Grace Paley. Her talk, like the voices in her stories, is colloquial, quirky, direct, energetic, funny. She has a thick "Noo Yawk" accent, chews gum, is anything but chic. After seeing her in public situations a few times, one gets the sense that she is acting down a little, a very smart, talented woman trying to make the point that this is all within the reach of the ordinary, that plain folks can write a book of fiction, change a diaper, and be arrested on the White House Lawn without having to change clothes or vocabularies. At the least, she is deliberately refusing (like John Hawkes) to play the role of the writer or to parade her learning: "I'm just like anyone my age. I read a lot of Joyce when I was a kid." She refers to the students in her audience not as students, or would-be writers, but as *writers*, and there are legends about how supportive she is of others who want help with their work. Anyone who writes is a writer, no trenchcoats, Ph.D.s or other paraphernalia are required.

In what follows, Ms Paley, taking part in the Women's Studies Program at the University of Minnesota, talks briefly about her work and then responds to questions from a group of writers. She clearly prefers the democratic interchange of questions and answers to a formal lecture.

PALEY: I've been in Minneapolis for a couple of days, and people have asked me certain questions. I would like to respond in some way to one or two of them. One question that often comes up is, "You're involved in all this political action and so forth and there really is little about it in your writing. How come?"

When people first asked me about this I'd worry about it a lot. I began to try to remember or think if I'd squeezed it in anywhere . . . what had I done? I began to feel a little bit guilty (not a lot guilty – you have to be born to that or trained to that early) and I'd better – and in my next few shots around – try something.

. . . But whenever I would go to work again I would find myself writing about some situation in ordinary life that really perplexed me, or terrified me, or terrified someone I knew. Finally I came to the conclusion that this really was part of my political life, and that though I didn't know this is what I was doing when I began to write about the everyday life of women around me, it seemed to me that that was one kind of political task, and that that moved in one direction, and the other happened in its own way. It certainly seems to me that both these forms of politics, the politics of the ordinary life of women and men, and the organizational or activist politics, are more and more closely related, especially in the disarmament and anti-nuke movement, which brings together our own personal flesh, our bodies, as women. . . . For a long time I thought about ourselves as women, and what places like Three Mile Island or Love Canal meant to us and to the children we bore and to our own flesh. Then I saw that this also involves men in a way I hadn't thought about before, not just in terms of their being affected but also in a sexual way. This unseeable, unsmellable radiation attacks particularly the foetus, the small growing child, and particularly the egg. I thought of the way in which people have always blamed everything on that poor egg. Anything that happened to that kid: something's wrong with the egg. Either it wasn't there, in that case there were no children; or it was its fault. I thought that was happening to men when they began to realize that they were really about to suffer something called rape, and that they may not want to think of it that way. But if they would think that what was happening to them was the violent if invisible entrance into their sexual bodies, and the attack upon the innocent sperm, if you want to call it that, as well as the pure egg, that men could begin to understand what rape was about also. They would have to begin to understand and see it that way. These are some of the ways I see the work I'm involved in as being all of a piece, none of it is separate, the literature or the politics, in any way.

Do you write when you have to? Or when do you write?

I write all the time, in a way. I'm not a very disciplined person. I write. I wrote yesterday, a little. Writing is a habit, among other things, and if you're a writer you'd better get into the habit. A lot of people don't realize that. When I'm writing a story then I'm really writing all the time, wholly involved in it. When I'm not writing a story, I'm still thinking. . . . Susan Sontag once said that she can't wait to get to a typewriter so she'll know what she thinks! And that's true for most writers, that you really have gotten this habit of thinking on paper. Until you do that all you have is a lot of junk in your head, a lot of stuff swirling around, and the paper is the place where you really begin to think.

An article on you in the paper the other day quoted you as saying that to do well in any art form one must be willing to look foolish. Does that come naturally? [Laughter]

No! No, nobody likes to look foolish. It can be one of the worst things in this world, the fear of embarrassment. I know people who are perfectly willing to sit down and get arrested, and go to jail. But the idea of knocking at the door of a neighbour's house is enough to kill them. They're so embarrassed. They think, oh, what do I look like . . . whereas they'd do quite dangerous things in another context. So fear of embarrassment, fear of sticking your neck out, fear of looking foolish, fear of writing in a way that nobody else is writing (I'm not talking about trying to be extraordinary or avant-garde) . . . there are people who stick through for twenty years. . . . I'll give you an example: William Carlos Williams. In his autobiography he says (I'll have to paraphrase this, he said it with a New Jersey accent), "Well, it looks like this guy T.S. Eliot has hit it real big with *The Waste Land*, it looks like that is the direction for literature." His next line is: "Now I know I will have to wait twenty years to be heard." So he did, he just kept doing what he thought was right, became a powerful influence, stuck to his ideas of the American language. But lots and lots of other people said, "Well, that looks like the way to go," and trotted off, cutting their roots as they went.

A writer may have to work for a very long time before gaining recognition. Do you have anything to say about that, particularly in terms of being a woman and having a family?

For those people who love the idea of being writers and being artists there's a great temptation . . . a lot of us grow up that way, a lot of little middle-class children, like I was, grew up thinking that was the great thing to be. Until I was fifteen or sixteen it was much admired in me, after which point my family turned against it very strongly. After that you're on your own. It has to stop being a question of being crazy about being an artist or being a writer. It becomes then a matter of subject matter. I'm saying that yet I really think a lot about language, all the time, how I write, it means something to me when I work, what sort of language I'm using. At the same time I think you have to come back to where you really are thinking about something. In this country (and probably in most countries) the word "message" is abhorrent. I don't like it myself, but I don't like it because it doesn't mean anything, but there you are, you're thinking about *something.* In my case it was specifically the life of the women around me, and my own at that time, which was the mid-fifties. Not only my life and the women around me, but also my aunts, you know? One of the first stories I wrote was about the female life of my aunt. I then had, in a sense, something to write about, if you want to call it that. What you find sometimes in class (I'm a teacher too), a kid will come up and say, "I want to write but I haven't got anything to write about." Well, that's true. And they may never. But what you do write about begins early in your life, and you somehow have that theme for a long, long time, and for me the theme has continued. And the reason for sticking with it, for persevering (I'm sticking with your question), is that it's still in your mind. It's not that the questions raised in the work are finally answered; life around you is changing all the time, you're getting older, and you're still thinking about these things, the subject matter, and the subject matter has really got you . . . in many cases, for life! And that's the fidelity to it that you have, and it's one that you can't help. And you have it when the children are small, and you have it when the children are bigger, and you have it when the children leave home, and there you are. Is that any kind of answer?

It certainly answers part of it. The other part was the more practical side. It's difficult for women with children to get time for themselves to do things. What is it like getting that time when, particularly as a beginning writer, it's a matter of taking the time from the children for work that has not yet got a great deal of social recognition?

I'd like to go on with that because that's an important question. A couple of women have asked that while I've been here. In the first place, for those of you who are young and don't know: it's very hard. Those of you who are older, and know: you know. But it's hard when the kids are small (if you have kids) and it's distracting. It's one of the reasons I myself have stuck with the short story. My mind has really gotten into short jumps, so to speak, and I think I was very often distracted in those days. I remember when I was a kid and I'd come home and my father was busy, everybody was told, "Shhhhh, Papa's busy" or "Papa's sleeping", or whatever, and we were quiet, very respectful and quiet, and sometimes angry, sometimes noisy and got put out again. Mostly we didn't turn against him, we didn't hate him. It seemed like a new idea to me, and to women I spoke to, to say, "Shhhhh, Mama's busy." Yet that's a perfectly legitimate way of dealing with it. One of the reasons women can't do it, even if their husbands are very helpful, is that society has told you that your egg is responsible for the child, and that you yourself are responsible for the life of the child, for what happens to the kid. The psychology of our life period has enforced that. In my generation particularly we were really sad a lot because we felt a lot was our fault. If there was trouble with the kids and we went to a psychiatrist we were told, "You're damn right, it's your fault." I don't think the present young women suffer to the degree that women in my time did, who were really in great pain about things like that. Truly parents do have something to do with the child, but all children, all people, you and me, are born in a certain time and in a certain place, and the society which brings you up, in which you are rich or poor, has an awful lot to do with what kind of a child you are. A society in which there is a war or drugs, or none of these things, conditions the life . . . the best care you give your kid will not save his life if he's sent off to war . . . so the idea that the mother can't take a couple of hours a day to work is really shameful and no woman should suffer that pain or that guilt. I'm always surprised because I think that young women are getting over that a lot and it was for us old folks that it was so hard, but I know that's not true. I think you should look to the world around you for who's bringing up your kid, because you're not.

How does it feel to go to jail? And does it accomplish anything?

I'll tell you what I think. I haven't really been in jail, in deep jail, if you want to put it that way. I've never been in longer than a week. I know lots of people who've been in a lot longer. The time I was there a week – I don't want to offend anybody – but I was fortunate I was there without a lot of movement people. The reason I was fortunate was that – if you go to jail that way – and that's the way that most people are afraid of – you should think of it as though you were given the opportunity to visit a foreign country, an oppressed nation, under severe repression, and the gift, the opportunity (if you're not going to be there two years and then go back again and again) the opportunity to not live in the Hilton Hotel of that nation, but to really live on the cell block, on the block, with the other people. If you look at it that way you begin to understand an awful lot that you never understood before. You never really understand what it means to hear those gates clang shut until you really have heard them more than a few times. Then you really know that there is an enormous population, a whole other nation out there, a country, that you have to think about and be concerned for. Whenever you're there to share it with them, it's not a bad thing. As for accomplishing anything: Nobody can really answer that question. I can only say that this last time we did this little action of standing on the White House lawn, really the littlest thing in the world that anybody could do, and unfurling this banner which said "No Nuclear Weapons and No Nuclear Power US or USSR", and other people in Russia did it, our friends from War Resisters did that also. . . . We just did this little thing, and it could have been a little thing, and the government if it had had any brains could have given us a ten-dollar fine or something, they made a great big thing of it, you know? When we were sentenced, my whole community came down, to see the sentencing. (I teach at Sarah Lawrence.) You could never have gotten three bus loads of people down to Washington on some abstract political issue. They all came down. The other ten people also had constituencies or friends or buddies. They all came down. There was another sit-down in front of the White House in which twenty-five people were arrested and they were released immediately, so our sentence was not repeated, which was pretty nasty. On the day of the sentencing, my Vermont affinity group (it was the middle of February, twenty degrees below) went and stood out on the Hanover Green and vigilled for us. And I had talked in Texas the week before and people did a vigil in Austin, Texas, of the same kind, with the same signs, giving out the same literature. There were many others in other places, those are just two. So I don't know what we accomplished. Had the government not responded in a silly manner we might not have accomplished so much, that's true. But . . . the members of my affinity group who had never been arrested before were among thousands who sat down at the Vermont Yankee nuclear plant, and 167 of them were arrested. I feel that it's all related. On the actions of each one of us, since we have two shoulders, at least two other actions can stand. Now whether we'll survive, whether all that can happen fast enough for us all to get through the next couple of years, we'll see.

You said that happened in the USSR also. What was the result there?

That's sort of funny, because they use their brains there. They tore up the banner, immediately, I mean within seconds, slashed it, took it off. Then pulled them in. Didn't arrest them, but ingathered them. Took them some place and yelled at them and told them not to do it any more, and then told them to go on with their journey. They were Americans, War Resisters League people.

You spoke of your Vermont affinity group. Do you live in New York City or Vermont?

I have to clarify this out of loyalty to my city which is always under such terrible attack from the rest of the country. I live in Vermont about every third year, but I am a New Yorker, and all my sad feelings are for my city. . . . For instance, there's going to be an action on October 29th [1979], it's called the Manhattan Project. People are coming in from New England and New York and . . . anywhere — you're all invited — and going to Wall Street, which is the centre of much of the disaster and horror throughout the world as well as here in the United States. . . . I work with a lot of New Englanders . . . their whole sense is that they're going to this awful place, this terrible evil centre. What they don't know is that they're going to a city where the people are as cruelly colonized as people anywhere in the world, and by that same power, and that the city itself has been bombed a hundred times over, if you looked at it, if you walked around and saw it, bombed a hundred times over, by things like . . . the Defence budget. All of the money that has gone into that has really destroyed most cities. I'd say. (I've not been around enough of this city [Minneapolis] to see anything but . . . lawns . . . but that's a typical New Yorker's view of out-of-town: it has a lot of lawns.)

I have a question about a character who goes through many of your stories: Faith. She almost seems detached from the action going on around her. Did you intentionally, consciously write that into her character, and why?

She certainly is like that in the very first story in which she appears, but I don't think she's like that in the later stories. But in that first story, what happened was I was going up to visit a friend of mine, and there she was, sitting there, and there were her two husbands, and they were both complaining about the eggs, just in the way the story began! It was exactly like that. She's one of my best friends and I often look at her and I don't think she realizes that I began "Faith" in her sixth-floor kitchen, but that's true, and she was rather cool about it. I think that that story was one of the first stories in which I saw a detachment from, not the story, but the story is about the fact that these four men, two boys and two husbands, are going to go about their business, and she's at the beginning of saying, "It's not my concern." But I don't think she does that afterwards, not so much, maybe now and then, but not when she's with other women.

In one of your stories, "The Long Distance Runner," you have a woman who leaves home for a while to go on a journey – she's not detached from her surroundings, but she's not playing her typical mother role to the boys, either. . . .

Oh, yes, some guy did a review of that, and he said, "What

kind of woman would it be who would go off running like that and leave her kids at home?" [*Laughter*] Well, the kids are kind of big, I think they're much older by that age, and that story has a kinda surrealistic touch to it. It isn't exactly your true story of running.

What touched that story off?

One of the things that touched it off was my going back to my own old neighbourhood, which I've described to you as being absolutely bombed out, and seeing my father and mother's house as it stood there. And through the invention of that "running", and staying with that family that now lived there, I tried to understand the way they were the same. The way they were together, the way they could live together. I tried to understand what happened, what it was like. It's hard for me to say what the story's about, only because I could be wrong. It's about something for you, and the reader is part of every writer's writing.

I sometimes find I write better in a depressed mood, do you find that? Do you write better in certain moods? It's almost like getting it out of your system – cathartic, you know what I'm getting at?

I know what you're getting at. No, I don't think so. I sometimes will have a fight with someone, especially a husband or someone like that, and go off and really *work* [*laughs*] but usually it doesn't turn out so hot. But I think that's a different way of using the work. I don't think it's wrong, it's just that as time has gone on for me, I don't use it like that. I really use it (work) to think about things . . . that I don't understand. More and more it helps me. It doesn't help me succeed in understanding but it helps me see what the world is really about.

Could you talk a little about what the short story should do, what your definition of it is, and has it changed for you over the years?

That's a hard question. A short story seems to me to be related to a poem more than it is to a novel. In some way it is almost as economical as a poem but has a little more happening inside of it. It works in that way. I teach "short story" but I can no more tell my class what a short story is . . . I know it's not a novel, so if they hand me a novel I can say, "This is a short-story class, I don't have time to read this." [*Laughter*] But I think the short-story form is marvellous and can do anything. It can be one page long, it can be forty pages. What it has to have in it is what is commonly called conflict in the trade, so to speak, but what I don't think of particularly as conflict, but what I think of really as the meeting of two events or ideas or experiences or sounds, and the story is really that sound. So you can do it very lightly, that can be the sound, or it can be really quite explosive, but without that you'd have what you'd call maybe a prose poem. Prose poems are a form I don't like much because they seem mostly to be written by poets who won't do the work of a story. A lot of poets don't like me to say that and I don't say it often. But they want to try their hand at prose and so they write the prose poem, and that doesn't do enough work for me, it doesn't do enough thinking. The cerebral nature, the real thinking nature of all this work is something that people don't want to . . . think about too much. So, there's a lot of that. So the main thing for me is that the story has to have these two, this coming together [*claps hands*] of two people, two events, two ideas, two sounds, two winds, whatever, and it's that bumping into which makes everything in the world happen, which makes energy, and it's that energy which is the sound, which is the story, and if you don't have it it's kind of weak and sloppy. And it has to have a beginning, a middle and an end, but the middle can be anywhere, it can be in the beginning, it could happen anywhere through the story. It has to have a shape, a rising and a falling. But no one is the boss of beauty or form, so what can happen in the future with all of this is . . . wonderful, and there's no law. There's a law for me, this minute. A lot of people say you can't write a really good didactic poem or story. I don't see why not. I haven't done it, I haven't seen it done, but someone will come along whose spirit understands that and it'll happen.

Does your reading influence your writing a lot?

I used to read a lot more than I read. For years I was what was called a big reader. Now I read a lot less. I think that everything I ever read is very influential on my writing and by that I mean the stuff you read from a very early age. The poets I read had a strong influence on me. But I think when we talk about influences we omit some of the most important influences on our writing, and they're never discussed really, and they're not literary at all. It may be why I feel close to Russian writers. It's because that's the language of my father and mother. So one of the major influences on my writing, I feel, is the street in which I grew up. I was out in it all the time. And the language of my family which was English and Russian and some Yiddish running back and forth a lot at great speed, and the life they talked about, the life they led. That language that I heard, and the language of the street, of the kids and also of the grown ups, who hung out in the street a lot in those days, that was as great an influence on my writing as anything I've read. As for form, that's another thing. I'm just like anyone my age. I read a lot of Joyce when I was a kid and those stories probably had a lot to do with my first ideas of form. I read a lot of Chekhov. I think those old things have influence. I don't think that anything you read . . . now, can strongly influence you, it can superficially do so but not really deeply.

Can you talk about the writing process in terms of your thinking? Do you "think on the page"? Do you do a lot of thinking about something before you begin to write? Or do you discover it as you write?

Well, I begin by writing something, and I just write it, and I may not even look at it for the next two years. So I have a lot of pages lying around. When I finish a story I start going through all my pages. I have all these pages. Some of them I'm amazed to see, are part of what I'm thinking about. We have this one head, so everything is just in there all the time. You write a few pages and then you . . . go away. . . . Which is, again, the distractable way that I work and it's not to be construed as a decent or honourable way of doing things [*laughter*] but I do think about things a long long time. When I'm really into a story I work very very hard on it. People ask me, How do you know when it's at an end? I just thought last week what was the answer: I know I'm at the end when I say to myself, How'm I going to end this thing? When I think I've finished it I then begin to go over it and I go over it for falsity mostly, and for lies. I just revise. I just think of it in those terms. I don't want anybody to think I just write when I feel like it, especially who are going to go into that line of work. You write also when you don't feel like it. It really is such hard work that if you are naturally lazy, like I am, you often feel like it, so you have to keep that in mind.

What do you think are the most commonly encountered lies that come up in your work?

Wanting certain characters to be something, or pushing them around. You get stuck with your own examples of things. The example I always use is how I got stuck giving some guy the wrong job. I was working on this story for a very long time and I just couldn't move ahead on it, and the reason was I'd given him the wrong job. He really was a taxi-driver and I think I gave him some sort of administrative responsibility somewhere. [*Laughter*] It really was bad, but until I realized that . . . I'd call that a lie. I wanted him in an office, you know? But once I'd got him out of the office, because he didn't belong there, then a lot of other things changed. There are other kinds of lies too. There are lies of language where you exaggerate, or put in a lot of adjectives, or you try to be high styled, or you try to be up-to-the-minute with what's being done. Those are lies. You can go through a story again and again and again until you can't change it any more, and then at the end . . . don't think in terms, is this story good or bad, you know? Because you never will know. What you can think about is whether it's true as you can make it. And then even if you think it's bad, you're probably wrong. "Oh, this lousy story I just finished." But it's what I had to say, and it's what I said, and everything in it is truly invented and true . . . then you probably have a good story.

Could you say something about humour in short stories?

The only thing I can say about humour is that if you're not funny you can't be. [*Laughter*] But did you want me to say something more serious about it? [*Laughter*] Humour I think by its very nature is out of place. I mean that. You have humour when you have great disparity.

Do you ever feel like your vision is losing steam? I don't mean in the writing sense, but your personal vision, the way that you live. And if that happens, where do you get support?

[*Pause*] Huh! [*Laughter*] That wasn't a joke, that "Huh".

Or do you just wait it out?

Yeah, I think so, I think you wait things out. If you're working hard on something and it doesn't seem like it's working out, you get kinda low. But you can't live in this world without friends. There are a lot of therapeutic devices nowadays to take the place of that, but . . . I don't know how I would live without my friends. I've felt that way from a pretty early age, and they have always been – through hard times – as supporting of me as I have been of them.

Ishmael Reed

Ishmael Reed was born in Chattanooga, Tennessee, in 1938, and grew up in the industrial city of Buffalo, New York, where he studied at the State University of New York. He has published several novels including *The Freelance Pallbearers* (1967), *Yellow Back Radio Broke-Down* (1969), *Mumbo-Jumbo* (1972), *The Last Days of Louisiana Red* (1974) and *Flight to Canada* (1976). He has also published poetry, including *Conjure* (1970) and *Chattanooga* (1973). He teaches creative writing at the University of California Berkeley campus.

Reed's books have been nominated for the National Book Award and the Pulitzer prize. He has won the National Institute of Arts and Letters award, and is widely recognized as one of the three or four best serious Afro-American writers working in the United States today. His work is often grounded in Caribbean or African mythology, but just as often in contemporary popular culture. The connection he makes in this talk between totemism in an Alaska tribe and Walt Disney's animal figures is typical of his range and of his refusal to compartmentalize or to accept the boundaries imposed by cultural decorum. He constantly rewrites the "official" versions of American history presented by textbooks, sending up its pieties through parody or dwelling on instances where flamboyant Blacks outwit their slavemasters. His books are funny, but he is no clown; his humour has an edge that has been sharpened by the emotions of four hundred years of racial injustice in the New World. The humour is buttressed by considerable historical knowledge and research, of the inspired rather than the systematic kind.

In recent years, prompted by his remarkable generosity toward other writers and his desire to bring about recognition of what he calls the fact of "multicultural America", Reed has become an editor and publisher himself, sponsoring the work of minority writers, not only Afro-American, but also Hispanics, Asian-Americans, and Native Americans. He began this cultural entrepreneurship in 1971 with Yardbird Publishing Company, which put out several fine issues of *Yardbird* magazine, and which continues to publish under the name of *Y-Bird*. He is director of Reed & Cannon, Inc., and a recent project was a huge volume called *The Before Columbus Catalog,* which gives picture, writing samples, and addresses for hundreds of minority writers, small press publications, etc.

He is a manic talker, building momentum from one sentence to the next, alluding frequently with good humour but obvious bite to the cultural wars that have occupied his adult life. Though he is very responsive, questions often seem superfluous – he knows where he's going and certainly needs no prodding.

What follows is excerpted from his remarks, some spontaneous, some prompted by questions, to a group at the University of Minnesota in 1979.

Welcome back to Minneapolis and St Paul.
REED: They always show me: "See over there, that's where John Berryman jumped off the bridge," every time I come back here. You go to Austin, Texas, they say: "Hey, you wanna see the tower that guy shot all those people from?"

I think we're in the middle of an American Renaissance in writing, and the good news can't get out because of a small group of men who dominate the politics and culture in this country, and their point of view reigns. It's always dangerous when you have one class, no matter what it's based upon, land, race, whatever, dominating the affairs of a country. It really is a multiculture; this country is not an extension of Europe, this is a multicultural nation. We may be influenced by other cultures – African, Asian, European – but there are forms and ideas here which are indigenously American, I believe. When I hear some of the pompous critics talking about craft and technique – most of them don't know enough about American forms to understand craft in a broad way. So I think what we have here is something equivalent to the Bourbons and the Romanovs. The small group of men use the same arguments, they say we don't come up to their standards. The Romanovs used the argument of divine right. They asked Nicholas, you know, before he got his, what made him think he was so terrific, and he said, you know [*laughs*]: "God." The argument about "standards" – I think it's the same kind of mystical argument. So I'm talking about parting what I call the "Romanov curtain" here. So many traditions – feminist, so-called "minority", experimental, and other kinds of writing – are not being projected, so we've organized to try to penetrate the Romanov curtain. White males in this country have a considerable amount of power; it's very hard to disagree with that. With only four per cent unemployment, they've managed what almost no other class in history has done economically.

The writing industry is similar, both in big press and small press, it's dominated by white males. They're the managers, the salesmen, they head the book reviews which support the works of other white males. Look at the leading American book review, *The New York Times*. I call it the *New York Times Colonial Book Review*. It has that Union Jack waving from its mast, from the pages. The British flag, and always the front-page review of somebody who's dead, preferably two hundred years or so, the longer the better. Instead of covering the writing that's going on in this country in different regions, among whites and blacks, and Native Americans, Asian Americans, or Hispanic Americans. I call the *New York Times Book Review* a weekly white male vanity sheet. This is not sour grapes, I get excellent reviews in the *New York Times*. Last time I got a review they had four drawings of me so expensive I couldn't afford them. This guy drew four pictures of me, I said, "Gee, great, how much are they?" I couldn't afford 'em. I realized a long time ago that I was a prominent token, and if I didn't know that, I'd be a casualty like a lot of people I know who started really believing the praise. When I was in New York in 1967, everything a black person did was praised, the bad stuff along with the good.

A lot of the worst political movements of this century started as cultural movements, if they didn't like the way you talk, they sent you to camps . . . I think the reason many Afro-American or so-called "Third World" people distrust writing is that they've been betrayed by writing so much. After slavery, I don't know whether it was naiveté or hope, Afro-American illiteracy went down drastically. You can look at the pictures that show ex-slaves of all ages learning to read and write. They thought there was some kind of magical power in it. But they were betrayed and lynched . . . nobody wanted them to be successful. You see what they got for writing and reading good English, and we still have their legacy where some critics write Victorian English, because of the debutantes who went down there to teach the slaves to read and write.

John Simon, on the Dick Cavett show recently, said that Blacks ought to speak and write standard English in order to get ahead. We have to wait for a future show for him to explain that the West and other parts of the country were taken from the Indians by men who spoke like characters in a Henry James novel. Or how Nelson Rockefeller, who thought "horrendous" was a term of praise, got ahead. According to Simon's ideas, most of our politicians and leaders shouldn't have gotten ahead. . . .

The kids who come into my classes (at Berkeley) are still writing some kind of nineteenth-century English. I have to cure them of it. I have to say to 'em, "Why don't you write normal?

Nobody still sounds like that. 'It is the cause, Desdemona' – nobody talks like that in this country!" If somebody's just being a custodian, a kind of janitor for some fetish, upholding tradition, then they should not have a big budget. It's been my observation that the writing departments and programs are becoming something to deal with, because they are neutral in a way, are beyond cultural politics. If you want all these super-race things, you know, you can go to the Afro-American Studies Department and they'll say, "We're the greatest." In the writing department, it's just writing, and that's why I think the writing departments are gonna get huge. I got thirty-seven students in my writing class. I'm carrying medieval prose, that's got three students in it. People are interested in writing, it's like a club. We have night classes, classes in town. There are other institutions off campus that can be used for this. . . .

You can get grants, you know, for artists in the community. *Before Columbus* did this in San Francisco last year. We had some readings. We brought the people out, had all different kinds of writers. One thing I found out is that poetry crowds prefer red wine to white wine. And we had a reading salesman, so you could buy the books right there after the reading. We've been doing distribution for twenty-two small press magazines, all the way from *The Unmuzzled Ox,* put out by Andy Warhol and some New York people, to *Maies,* a Chicano magazine coming out of San Diego. We go all over to book fairs and stuff.

I began to see something was happening, that we were really getting somewhere with a new definition of American writing as multicultural writing, when I went to Paris last year, lugging all these books. There was a conference, I didn't even know what it meant, turned out it was a conference on the New Novel. Well, if they say I'm writing the New Novel, fine, I'll go to Paris for that! [*Laughter*] We put all the magazines on a table, and these people at the Sorbonne from all over the world came to look at these magazines. They had never seen American literature represented in anything other than monocultural terms. So we're trying to do practical things and we're working in a good way with whites on our board. If I sound enthusiastic or euphoric about this, it's because I am. I think that the Renaissance is already here, and that the good news is being withheld. Even the big publicity machines will embrace us sooner or later, because you can't miss it. By the year 2000, California may well be a fully multicultural state, with a majority of Hispanics.

You create, or you have in the past, particularly with Yellow Back Radio, *black heroes and cowboys who do a lot of wild things a lot of unusual things, things you might want to see but which aren't there in reality, are they?*

I wrote the book in reality. It's based on real life and on a mythology I was interested in at the time, a mythology which seems as valid to me as Greek mythology. I was working on an international mythology, in an international aesthetic. These things are well known in Brazil and Haiti and Cuba, and are slowly coming into this country. And I think they can be used for practical results. In *Yellow Back,* I was experimenting with Vodoun mythology, just as a Western poet would experiment with Greek mythology. There are a lot of these guys in Connecticut who write about Zeus, but you don't see them out in the back yard offering libations to the gods. What I wanted to do was to create something out of my own psychology, my own tradition, my own heritage, and I think that's healthy for me.

In one of your essays, "Shrovetide in Old New Orleans", you said that there was a lot of jargon and abstruseness about the political movements in the 1960s and that you became cynical very early. Could you give more details about the things that happened to you?

If you weren't writing in their way or living their lifestyle, you got ostracized.

Are you at liberty to say who "they" are?

That's not important because all of them have gone to the Republican Party, and they own Mercedes cars. They have all abandoned those positions. I don't want to embarrass anybody. Some of them were in this particular line in the sixties and now they're making all-American speeches and telling people to read Virginia Woolf and all that stuff. But it was different then. And we had a lot of battles about that because I always like a good scrap, I guess, and combat. I think my sign is Shango, the warrior. They would make demands upon us, and we found them unacceptable. There was a lot of letters back and forth, name-calling, and stuff like that. But I found that to be boring. Intellectual pastimes. I decided to start to do things, and I thought you'd be more effective doing that.

Were you a part of what is now called the Black Arts movement or Black Aesthetic movement?

Sure, son, I founded it. My own experience with Black Arts was with *Umbra Magazine* in the early sixties. I came from Buffalo; I didn't know anything about it. I didn't know anything about politics. I came from Buffalo, New York, and nobody cared anything about politics. The only politics we had were Democrats and Republicans. And they would run every two years or every four years. And when I went to New York, these people were intellectually aware. And they used terms like "nationalism". So we all lived in an apartment. And Marcus Garvey's kids used to come down there and all these people. We were writing, experimenting. Calvin Hernton. (I just published his book *Medicine Man*.) He's probably one of the early founders of the Black Poetry thing. He's writing the language that people talk in the streets and about urban life. Like he wrote poems about Harlem. He lived in Harlem. And he wrote poems about the streets and they're written in the language that people in the streets would talk. And that to me was new because I had come out of the university where they had told me that I was smarter than everybody and they thought that I was speaking like Clark Kent. So I was writing all of this stuff with mythological stuff in it, influenced a little bit, as much as I could understand, by Ezra Pound, Eliot and all this stuff. And then I ran into these guys who were speaking a more basic type language, and then, of course, it influenced my stuff. And that was the beginning of Black Arts. And the people in it, we had an apartment together on the Lower East Side, and LeRoi Jones at that time was in California. He was calling us revolutionaries.

What year was that?

It was 1963, late 1963. And he came out to California to deliver a lecture with Ginsberg and Rexroth and all those people and referred to us on WBAI radio station as revolutionaries. When he came back, the people I had been associating with, my roommates, moved uptown with him – Charlie Patterson and Rolland Snellings (Askia Muhammad Touré) who wrote recently that I was in league with the Rockefellers. Somewhere. Look at my coat. The buttons are coming off. They all moved uptown and then I heard that they were doing something called Black Arts. They didn't want us up there. I went to read on the night of its opening, the Black Arts Repertory Theatre of Harlem. So that's what I know about Black Arts. All of those guys were very smart – Bill Light, Baraka, all of them. And the other poets kind of connected that up with the occult, you know, witchcraft – Black Arts. It was very scary. You know, someone comes along and says, "Black Arts! I'm going to get you!" So that's what I know about that. And then I moved to California in 1967. I understand some of the Black Arts stuff started out there in California too. Somebody's going to have to do some more work on that.

How did you discover Vodoun as a system?

From a painter. Not from writers. We all were around musicians and painters, so we were influenced by more writers in

New York. Joe Overstreet, a painter, introduced me to that. I was in a loft, and I asked him what the symbols were and he told me what they were. The *vèvè*. And then I started reading material about it. And what I always tried to do was to put together disparate material that nobody would ordinarily connect – collages. . . . So I said, what you do is you take this Vodoun system and put it together with this cowboy thing, because I had read somewhere that the spirits or the loas were horsemen. They ride you. Maya Deren, one of the writers on Vodoun, wrote a book called *The Divine Horsemen.* So I said that this is ready-made for a cowboy book. I was going to call it *Horsemen.* So that's how these two things came together. You see? I was always interested in popular forms, taking popular forms and doing something different with them. Like *Mumbo-Jumbo.* It's a detective novel and a mystery. And there are a lot of esoteric things – mysteries – in it, but at the same time it is a detective novel because there are people consciously looking for clues. And there are villains, culprits, and this kind of thing. It's a lot of detective work in there. One guy wrote a thing in *Popular Library,* or *Popular Culture Concept,* that it was the first experimental detective novel. I was very glad to be in the same volume with Dashiell Hammett and Raymond Chandler.

Is that what you consciously created it as?

Sure. I know what I'm doing when I start this stuff out. We were around artists, painters. We weren't really interested in telling stories. But the Vodoun thing, I guess I kind of started it, and other people picked it up and everything. Now it's all over the place with these sonaria people moving into Cuba and all over New York. So now they correct my pronunciation. This new generation say this is not the name of that god. I tell them that they are all caught up in ritualistic paraphernalia, that all of that stuff is not important. What do you do with it in the real world? That's what's important. Not how many gods you can identify with or what they do or what their characteristics are and what their diets are and all this kind of stuff. We did some odd stuff. We did a radio program with Victor Hernandez Cruz, the Hispanic poet, and I did some stuff on the radio about a month ago in California on Emana, the goddess of the sea, the night before the eclipse. And we told everybody to have champagne next to the radio and candles. So you don't have to join some crazy organization or cult to have some kind of spiritual belief. The thing about Vodoun is that you can do it in your own home. So it's not an organized thing. It's not like this thing of "Follow me to Guyana" or "Follow me to the Promised Land." None of this bullshit. It's different. So I did stuff like that with it. But I'm not an expert on it. It's a lifetime study – don't even know if I *want* to be an expert on it. What I try to do is capture the essence of it and try to use it in my work and in my business. What really got me in the business was the HooDoo people in New Orleans who were in the business. Before that I thought every Black person was a marxist. I was living East. I thought everybody was a marxist intellectual. I started reading this material and saw that these people had beauty shops and all this, and they sold their charms and amulets. They were actually doing things in the community. And so that's what we do. We publish books. . . .

The first book we published we put the Erzulie *vèvè*, the heart with the dagger, on the cover, and we threw a party for it. And coincidentally, it was held on the same floor where they were having a Haitian show. So this Haitian painter said, "What are you doing here?" Some kind of connection. So somebody said I take that book everywhere I go. Well, that's an amulet. An amulet is something you carry on your person. So we just expanded that definition. We are not interested in diet, purity, or orthodox stuff. So why don't you go into learning your Yoruba? No, none of that. I'm trying to use it as in daily life. And that's what it's used for. Blacks use it in daily life. And they sing it. I mean Black people get in the car and they turn on the radio. You don't have to go around poking for attention. Just turn the radio on. They say that Black English is not communicating with anybody. Barry White must be getting across. Earth, Wind and Fire – millions of people buy their records. They must be communicating. So it all comes out of the same tradition.

I note that in your early poetry there was a very direct statement of VooDoo and HooDoo experience but in Chattanooga *it seems a little less direct.*

I am moving away from it. If you start off with a system that has not been used that much before in literature you kind of hammer it home, say a lot of author intrusions and some of that stuff, you know, where the lecture comes. Reader, now this means . . . Blah! Well, it's ridiculous. So now I am able to blend that into my work. You don't have to know it to know that it's there. It's there, but you can read it without all this background.

What are you working on now?

As a matter of fact, I am going in another direction, based upon animal figures and materials, ideas I've gotten from Native Americans. What I've done is to start out using it in a play. Somebody bought the options to *The Freelance Pallbearers* which I wrote when I was in my twenties and it's ten years later. So I didn't write the same thing. It is very difficult to meet yourself ten years ago. You're a different person. So I got stuck on it and said I can't write this thing over again. So when I went to Alaska, I saw these totems out there in a forest. That put me on to the frog clan, wolf clan, the raven clan, and all these different ideas symbolized through animals. I said that this must be something that I could use. I thought of Disney. Walt Disney uses totems. I bought my kid a Mickey Mouse. Man, you should have seen that, a big Mickey Mouse. I said you may as well buy an archetype. Disney hit with that. And then when I discovered, when I went out to California – you see how all of these things are connected in whatever you do – I did this anthology of California poetry, and I found that the early Indians were into totem things and so that led me back into Afro-American folklore where I got these rabbit figures, Shine, folklore – the real stuff. Not the elegant or existential novel in the twentieth century. I got into a lot of trouble because I reviewed Levine's *Black Culture and Black Consciousness* where I said that the typical story among the masses of people was obscene and funny, and that this other stuff was probably aberrational. Why did I say that? They came out of the woodwork. The marxist novel and the elegant, well-crafted novel were probably aberrational, and the real stuff was probably bawdy and outrageous. You see that in native American stuff; you see that in pagan works. Read those coyote things, man, they are really — well, it's not for mixed company. It's like, well, I don't want to say that, not these days. It's pretty raunchy.

A lot of these things are fragments and they have never been developed. And it's like somebody going back into their folklore, taking these characters and ideas and using them. Stuff that has been assembled over the years by anonymous writers as some stuff has been done.

Do you tend to use them in contrast to the condition of where you're at today?

Yes. Right. Totems are universal. They're in all cultures, I think. At least most cultures. So when I was able to go look at different experiences I could see that I had a lot in common with this instead of the standard Western traditional thing that white writers are abandoning. We have people who write in eighteenth-century, nineteenth-century English. When Charles Bukowski is writing about Los Angeles, you know what I mean? Knocking them dead and drinking beer. So that's what I'm into next. Whether I'm successful or not – I've tried that already. I'll read some poems tonight in a series and I'm trying it in a play, using it in a play. We have animal characters and human characters in the same play.

Can you describe for us the New National Poetry?

It's the sum total of all the different writings and different cultures that we have in the United States goes to make up the National Writing.

Not many of the works are in anthologies. I mean, look at one of them. After I finished *Califia,* I just felt like, as I said in the introduction, the man who entered Tut's tomb and watching all of that stuff that was for centuries buried in what I call Golden Darkness. And they asked him, "How does it look?" And he said, "It looks wonderful!" And that's what I felt. There was nothing richer than to read all those traditions and cultures together in the same book, in alphabetical order from all over time. From the 1840s down to 1977. With separate introductions. Simon Ortiz, Bob Callahan, and all these people. Because I see the Afro-American culture, we're taking the leadership in this. We're no longer on the defensive saying, "Here we are. Could we integrate? What do you want us to do? Gonna be mad at each other?" We're taking the leadership in this. So we get a Nigerian General come to our office in New York last month. He had heard about *Y-Bird* in Nigeria, our books in their universities. The State Department brought a Turkish writer down to our little dingy office, and she took all those books. She wasn't interested in the standard stuff. She bought Victor Cruz's book, the Native American material we had, and a variety of stuff. And she was really amazed because nobody had ever told her or they had never considered that there were these many people, these many cultures active in the United States. And if you read the *Times* or these others you wouldn't know that at all. So that's what I meant by that and I think that we can take the leadership in that. We are the ones who are like the catalysts for this right now.

Do you think that the academically-trained critics will be able to support what you are trying to do?

Its success is not dependent upon them. All success does not depend on them. Matter of fact we have information for them which is a turnabout. . . . I think a lot of the academics have been out; they usually follow. You know, it took a long time for them to teach Eliot. It look them a long time to accept Eliot and people like that in the universities. There is a lag because of their distrust of writers and of artists, but I think that this is changing. That is, some of our best writers, you know – John Barth, I like his work – some of the good writers come out of academia, but there does seem to be a tradition of distrust where people will not follow any discipline. You never know how they are going to come to class dressed. They won't follow the rules. And I think that the American University is going to have to change; I think that it is changing.

How about yourself in the academic situation? How do you feel and how do you operate as a teacher on the staff at Berkeley?

Well, that's okay. We had a big fight two years ago where they offered me tenure and they weren't able to get it through. And, of course, I did not exploit their embarrassment because I did not want to get into a confrontation thing with them. I figured I could get it another way. So, they created a new post for me. I'm a senior lecturer, and the last senior lectureship they gave was to Lionel Trilling.

With tenure?

It's as close to tenure as I want. I'm not good at committees. I wouldn't want to be on committees there. I teach one course. I have an arrangement with them. And I move around. Like I'm going to Yale in the Fall. . . .

But I'm still there [*laughs*]. I don't plan to go away. And I have huge classes. . . . Plus I give those kids jobs. I give those students jobs. I don't just leave them in a rarefied world. I give them actual work to do. My business manager is a former student of mine. I took him out of the unversity and he's running my business. He's taking courses in financial marketing, lay-out, graphics, and all this. I had five students working with me on the anthology and plus we published a book out of the classroom. I'm able to do more than just teach somebody. I take them through the whole process. I teach them how to deal with the world – argue with the printer, and how to get estimates, how to do lay-outs. So they learn practical things.

If you don't think you have to be macho, how do you perceive manhood?

That's a difficult question. I think it varies from individual to individual. I'm just looking at all this destruction that this macho foolishness is causing. Of course, I grew up in a patriarchal household. Women who didn't behave correctly, you told them to shut up and sit down, go somewhere; you know what I mean? Those were the kinds of models we had. It takes a long time to unlearn that stuff. So when I wrote that slave book, and I still had some of those attitudes, I said, How can I relate to people as slaves? It's a contradiction to behave as a slave master and at the same time require that other people won't behave that way. Don't you see? It's caused a lot of turmoil and confusion. So that's why I think it's difficult. But I don't know about manhood. People should take that as it is. I don't think that you have to be a real macho daredevil to be a man. I think macho is for the birds. Not only do men get destroyed over macho, women and children do too. I'm not talking about the Hispanic *machismo*, which is a brotherhood, a way of relating to people. I'm talking about this John Wayne stuff which is going to get all of us killed if somebody doesn't stop it.

Some of the female characters in Louisiana Red *are very stereotypical. Why did you do it this way?*

I don't know about stereotypic. I think that there is such a thing as the classical bitch both among men and women, and a bitch personality. Matter of fact, Calvin Hernton wrote a book entitled *The Male Bitch,* and I don't think that thousands of years experience can be maybe wrong that much. I was talking about a type of a person, and I based it originally on Antigone and the idea which people lost – I've got a bunch of people reading Sophocles. These professors, they've got these kids reading Sophocles, which is ironic: Antigone transfers to modern times as Minnie the Moocher and a present-day revolutionary. There are women like that in the real world. I don't see how there is conflict between my ideas about the macho thing and the characters I portray unless I write an essay. A lot of people got upset about the dialogue between Minnie the Moocher and Papa Labas. But he was a Legba figure and a patriarch, African figure, an old man. And he's a patriarch. There's such a character as a patriarch and there is such a character as a bitch.

Many women who read the book, Toni Morrison and people like that, didn't get upset about the portrayals. People who heard it second-hand or heard it on talk shows or read the paper that this is what the book was about got upset. A lot of the people didn't even read the book. There are a variety of women in that book – Miss Better Weather and the Sisters. There are different types of women. Somebody called it a misogynous book. It's like sometimes in the sixties we called people racists whether it was true or not. Sometimes it's just a convenient way of getting out of an argument [*laughter*], a lazy way of getting out of an argument. Now the Black male is being made the scapegoat for the women's movement. . . . The frustration I see for Black men is that there's nowhere for them to express their point of view. For a Black man these days, it's a little like eavesdropping about your own fate. Like listening really close through the kitchen door at the plantation – "Hey, they gonna sell old John down the river tomorrow!"

I think that something happens to groups when they become frustrated and really cannot analyse power in the country. They

cannot analyse people who hold power in this country because
they're sleeping with them. What would happen if Lenin was
sleeping with the Czar? Fighting the guy all day and then with
him at night. It's difficult. I can understand the problems. So
what they do is seek a scapegoat. Every group does that. They go
so far and then Jimmy Carter says, "Get out the White House. I
don't even want you here," before he put Rep. Conyers out.
Wilson put Monroe Trotter out the White House. Told him to
get on out the White House. "How dare you come in here!" Put
Bella Abzug out the White House. So how do you analyse that?
So women in their frustration strike out, so now it's the Black
male. So now they have to seek a scapegoat and the tendency is
to pick on somebody weak who doesn't have all that much
power. So that's what's happening.

*I think that's false, though. What you're saying about the
women's movement is not true. I don't think they're using the Black
man as a scapegoat.*

Well, Susan Brownmiller wrote a book *Women Against Rape*
in which she exaggerated the Black man's proclivity to rape and
said Emmett Till was some kind of demagogue, a fourteen-year-
old kid who just looked at some woman the wrong way.

I don't think that Black men are responsible for the women's
problems in this country because the Black men don't have any
power. Why don't these white women writers get to analysing
what's really wrong with the country and then they'll be radical-
ized? A lot of this stuff is like middle-class stuff. And Gloria
Steinem and those people, a lot of those people are eating well,
Susan Brownmiller, they're authors, they get big cheques. . . .

There are a lot of people in this country who are starving. And
some people accuse feminists of diverting attention from the real
problem in this country, which is widespread malnutrition and
hunger. I got put down for talking about Haiti, saying Haiti is not
all that bad. Most people are starving in Haiti and I said, Well,
shit, if I want to see somebody starve, I can go down the street in
my hometown in Berkeley. I can see somebody with malnutrition
right here.

Now this is a country where about forty million people go to
bed hungry every night, and this country, which is the most
powerful country in the world, can't feed its forty million people.
How do you expect a country like Haiti which doesn't have
anything . . . ? They don't have resources, bad farming has
screwed up the soil. There is nothing down there. Maybe a little
tourism. Most of the people do their independent kind of
industries which is what impressed me about the iron market.

And what impressed me also was that I did not see the kind of idleness that you see up here in the Northern cities where thousands of people stand on the corner. You go to Harlem right now and you'll see men, women and children standing on the corner with nothing to do. At least down there they're busy. I said I don't know anything about the politics, but I do have some criticisms of the dictatorship in the essay. I said that dictatorships are bad because you can't get all the points of view when you get one man rule. And other criticisms of dictatorships are in the essay. I went to the galleries and I went to museums and got into the folklore. And if my job was to write about malnutrition and hunger, I could do that right here. I could go to New York. Got a ghetto here? People are starving right in this town I'll bet you, right here in Minneapolis. Why have to go all the way to Haiti to write about hunger?

The readership of books, paperback and hardbound, in America, is basically a middle-class readership, is it not?

I don't know. I've never done any studies on it. When I go around the country, I find that people of all classes and races read my stuff.

But don't you think that it's more middle-class or students?

I don't know how you would ascertain the figures. Do you mean people who buy books or people who read books second-hand or books that are passed around?

Let me put it this way. I don't see the brother on the street reading Mumbo-Jumbo. *I would like him to.*

Plenty of them read it. *Louisiana Red* I was surprised. People go to libraries. I saw Stanley Crouch saying in the *Village Voice* that the audience was largely white. I think that's an assumption that nobody has done research on in marketing.

I didn't say "white"; I just said "middle-class".

Yellow Back Radio Broke-Down was introduced to a lot of Black students by their parents. I get that from someone saying, "My folks said I ought to read this book." So, it's hard to tell who's reading. I get my books over in Japan and in Spain – *Mumbo-Jumbo* especially because it's dealing with an international aesthetic, that people may not know here. . . . One guy said he found *Pallbearers* in the middle of the Gobi Desert. He found these kids with camels and they had a copy of *Pallbearers*. You never know who's reading.

You were talking before about how obscene the coyote tales are. Are you trying to elevate people's tastes?

I'm saying they're less refined than the kind of stuff that passes as Afro-American literature in the twentieth century. The Shine stories, the signifying monkey stories are very raunchy, very down to earth. And they remind me of the native American tales which are the same way.

Do we want to refine that or just recapture that and get it out more or what?

I'm not trying to refine people's tastes, obviously. [*Laughs*] And my stuff is not distributed that well.

You do want to educate people?

Well, I don't know about that. I'm not a commercial success. I would say that. We do the best we can. And what I do is like since I am, I would like to cover the territory that hasn't been covered very much. If I see some mythology or folklore back there, I'm going to use it. If nobody's used it before, I'm going to use it; I'm going to develop it. And whether it raises people's consciousness, I don't know about that; people really may be smarter than you are. I don't know about raising their consciousness or educating them, but if that happens, then that's good too.

Reading and writing are taught badly in the schools. My oldest daughter Carla, because her mother kept her out of school for religious and political reasons, I taught her how to read in six months. And she wrote a novel. I sent it to Random House and they said that it was better than anything that I had ever submitted. She said, "Dad, maybe I'll take your place." Well, I took interesting stuff, I took the *New York Times Op. Ed.* and just threw it at her. "Now you read everything in there and tell me what those words mean." We'd drill every day. And then she started writing and now she can write. So I can teach anybody how to read and write. But when you get into the future pluperfect and all this mystery, this esoteric stuff, it turns people off from writing. When you use dull material, it turns them off too from writing. People can learn to read and write by practising. And I've found that talent in common – it's not confined to a few guys living on Long Island that you read about in *People* magazine. So I think that there should be a new way of doing it. I think that more writers should be in the schools because I think that writers can teach reading and writing. They may not be able to teach tradition, ideology. You know, Wordsworth, Southey or Mouthey or somebody like that. Know where Southey lived? – in England. Those guys go to England. Those guys from my department at Berkeley go to England. "I was in *London* last summer!" Me – I'm looking at Detroit and Cleveland. I'm going to Los Angeles trying to get me some material out of there.

Alan Sillitoe

Alan Sillitoe was born on 4 March 1928 in Nottingham, the son of a tannery worker. He worked in a bicycle plant and a plywood mill, and was a lathe operator, before being sent to Malaya as a Royal Air Force radio operator in 1946. In Malaya, he began to write poems and stories, as well as the draft of a first novel later destroyed. He became tubercular, and while living in Majorca on a small disability pension was advised by Robert Graves to "write about Nottingham. That's what you know." This helped Sillitoe to find his own voice, and the result was *Saturday Night and Sunday Morning* (1958) and *The Loneliness of the Long-Distance Runner* (1959). These books established him as a social realist, the novelist of the English working class and a sympathetic chronicler of its somewhat inchoate rebellious impulses. He has since written of more intellectual and explicitly political rebels, but has continued to write poetry and to transcend the narrow definition of social realism, as the title of his book *Shaman and Other Poems* (1968) indicates. He has published many volumes of short stories and poetry, and has done screenplays for films of his own work. His more recent novels include: *A Tree on Fire* (1967), *A Start in Life* (1972), *Flame of Life* (1974) and *The Second Chance* (1981). The following extract from an article in *The New Statesman* on Alan Sillitoe, by Alan Burns, focuses on Sillitoe's working methods. The discussion that follows amplifies the matters touched on in the article.

Noticing a slim, dark man waiting at a bus stop, Alan Sillitoe wrote in his notebook: "The rabbi and his slender wife stood at the bus-stop." He read this to me while talking about the origins of his ideas and images, and how he constructs his novels. The note about the rabbi was predictable: an excellent social novelist creating a character, giving a man's slimness to a fictitious wife. But in marrying [Alan's wife, the poet Ruth Fainlight, is also slim, dark, Jewish] his inner consciousness to external reality, Alan relies on instinct. A similar note, written in the spring of 1957, generated his best-known book. Back in England for a few weeks after five years away in France and Spain, he was living in a cottage at Manuden near Bishops Stortford when he saw a runner go by the window and wrote: "the loneliness of the long-distance runner" on a sheet of paper. In May, he went back to Spain. The following year, in Alicante, packing his papers for

another journey back to England, he found the line about the runner. He sat down in the middle of the packing and wrote half the story. At home in England the other half was finished in a few days.

The poetic perfection of *The Loneliness of the Long-Distance Runner* derives from the impenetrable flow of a "received" work. This cannot happen all the time, but a short poem like "The Poem Left by a Dead Man" and the fine short story "Mimic" still "come" in the same way, and the "received" is still crucial to Alan Sillitoe's writing. We talked about magic, mysticism, and the sources of inspiration, though Alan's interest in these subjects is balanced by his hard-headedness, his reticence concerning direct self-revelation, and by his insistence on the need for control or "centralizing", to use his word for it.

BURNS: *Do you prefer to leave the question of creativity "in the shadows"? Do you feel that to push it too hard would be damaging, making heavy weather of a thing that should be left to find its own rhythm?*
SILLITOE: I don't know, I don't think it's damaging particularly. Maybe I don't think it's damaging because I don't think anyone can find out much about it. If they could find out, anyone could program a computer to turn out exactly what I'm turning out. Because if you can find the mechanics of a thing, you can superimpose those mechanisms on a machine.

We're talking about the mechanics of consciousness and imagination and memory. . . . So I agree there's no need to worry about computer competition, as yet. But the fact remains that the beginnings of the Long-Distance Runner *involved a bit of magic, didn't they?*

Yes, they did, but if you say it's magic, people will think, la-la-la fucking la-la, you know? Have you read this work by Mircea Eliade on Shamanism, a marvellous six-hundred-page book. It's too big for me to synthesize, but I connect it with the writer's situation: the seven-year apprenticeship, the access through secret processes to the law and history of the tribe, the visionary brooding power. Obviously it's not all the same, but the inspirational part . . . when the Shaman is called into a tent to see someone who's sick, and he faith-heals them, or recites a certain portion of his tribal law over them, or he suddenly says something which comes from he doesn't know where, such as a combination of flowers, and this is something he's never used before but it comes into him now . . . where it comes from he doesn't know, he wasn't responsible, you see. But he had the training to make it likely that this body, this knowledge, would shoot into him when he was going half into an epileptic fit. This is all in a way bullshit, but it's got a connection. We get back to Graves's *White Goddess* and his grammar of myth. But let's face it, I don't feel anything special. People have said it must be marvellous to write books as if I'm a special sort of person. Well, I'm not, you see, because I don't claim any responsibility. How can one be responsible? I'm responsible for the bad stuff, but I'm not responsible for the good.

Then how did you come to write the good stuff?

I was helped, shall we say, by something I don't know about. The bad stuff, I was too conscious of *work*, and grinding the stuff out and making it match and latch and connect.

"Helped by something I don't know about." There's a strong come-off-it instinct in you which shies away from the mystical, and yet you must talk of it.

I only shy away from the mystical in order to give the mystical more chance to get at me. I'm in no way opposed to it. If I were to be a mystic, I would do it in real terms; I don't flirt with anything.

So you keep quiet about it in order to let it happen?

Yes, in order to keep the hypocrisy at bay, and in no way become entangled. I keep mysticism in its place.

This "inspiration" or whatever we call it is very intensely sought by the many people who wish to latch on to it. They take extreme measures to get in touch with it, various drugs, frenzied and self-destructive efforts. You have no need of that?

I've never taken drugs. I smoked a cigarette once, hash, but that was nothing. I never take drugs, LSD, anything.

Why?

[*Sighs*] Well, I refuse to, for many reasons which may not be the real reasons. My way of putting it is that it would interfere with my sense of self-respect. When you write, you have to be ice-cold, you have to have nothing foreign in your body if you're trying to write a poem or a paragraph. All your native, innate faculties have to be your own in order to see the most clearly and with precision. I know what a state of intoxication is because I've been drunk of course, and it's wonderful, terrific to be drunk now and again, one needs it, as a blackout, but not to do this, not to write.

You need all your wits about you?

What I need is centralizing. Some people can write marvellously when they're drunk. I need to be centralized. Call it right tight little self if you like but the more centralized I am the deeper I go. I have this trouble: I'm not an intelligent person. I'll qualify that, I've never been conscious of being particularly intelligent. What I mean is that normally my bloody mind is fuzzy and I'm not sharp. Mathematical puzzles and conundrums fuck me around awfully, so I've got to keep my brain as sharp as it possibly can be, and it's not the sharpest under alcoholic stimulant.

Have you tried to write drunk?

I've been sploshed a bit and a poem's come to me and I've written a bit, sometimes it's been good and at other times trash. But being drunk means that in any case my energy goes. I could write for half an hour, but no more, and that alone makes it not worthwhile.

You don't think this avoidance of drugs is connected with a reluctance about self-revelation? Do you think your fiction is a form of self-protection, a way of avoiding confrontation with yourself?

It's something I've thought about quite a lot. If you want to get from A to B and between them there's a wall, you can either tunnel under it, which is going to take a bloody long time, or get ten sticks of dynamite and blow a hole in it, with LSD, say. Now I'm quite prepared to tunnel under it if it takes ten years, rather than blow a hole through it. Because the process of tunnelling is as important as getting through.

But is it true that your work is a form of self-defence?

There's a certain core of truth in that. I think the world is such a bloody terrible place that one creates one's own boundaries and notions. You create your own continent. I think certainly I may be trying to do that, but at the same time, one pushes forward. You extend your boundaries. You may not extend them, you may go deeper into the earth.

I want to come back to the question of how you "tap your instinct". A clumsy phrase, but do dreams and fantasies come into it? Do you deliberately use dreams the way some writers do?

I don't use dreams. I dream. I remember them sometimes, sometimes I don't, but when I do remember them I don't record them. I think dreams are unimportant.

Forgive me, but I'd call that another avoidance. To my mind, dreams are indisputably of profound importance.

Let me qualify. I said dreams are unimportant. Now, they're not unimportant. What I do is, deliberately, as a matter of policy, I don't pay attention to them. If I remember them, I note them in my brain and say: "Yes, yes, I dreamed of that last night."

Dreams are of such importance that they should be left alone, so that they surface in such a way that you can use them without their being recognized as dreams. But I wouldn't use them directly because they are actually bubbles of raw material bursting on the surface of your consciousness. I don't want to give the impression I'm totally supine. Of course you "wait for it", but at the same time one brings it out. One has certain subtle mechanisms for bringing out stuff, but only when it's ready. You have to do your bit as well, you don't just wait with you legs up or anything, you work as well. I tend to exist on that borderline between daydreaming and thinking. It's very fertile: I mean, where do one's thoughts pop up from?

That's what I'm trying to find out.

Even more: abstract thoughts, not necessarily images, faces, or bits of dialogue, come from this borderline. I don't really know when I'm thinking or when I'm musing or when I'm day-dreaming. My waking hours take place in a merging of these three states, whatever they are individually. But we can't define these states, or scientifically separate them. It's like oil and water, vinegar and oil, they swirl around when you stir them up.

The difficult bit to grasp is the way consciousness travels along at different levels simultaneously, and the levels are interchanging, and that's all happening in time as it goes along. Hard to grasp, and very difficult to put across.

This is where you get the great separation between life and art, of course. Your mind is operating on three or four different levels, but anything you write has to have a clear, distinct, in-controvertible line about it.

Well, your work does. It has that linear force, that strong con-struction, very strong narrative.

It's very difficult to bring that line out you see.

You've deliberately avoided impossible complexity? Joyce had one way and Proust another, of trying to express this interweaving. The third way, that interests me, is the fragmented way, the attempt to disconnect rather than connect, to evoke the complexities by the space between the images. Is the distance between complex consciousness and simplified art bothersome to you? Does your own work ever disappoint you because it doesn't express more of the complexity?

I have this prejudice, call it what you will: what you read in print has to be fairly easily understood. This is something which I can't eradicate. I could begin to experiment in a much more lavish way if I wished, but somehow I don't want to. I want to maintain whatever clarity I can produce. Because finally, one of the greatest qualities of a writer — I'm telling you this, but you know — is patience. Right? One's always in the position of wanting to jump the gun, to get on ahead. And to me it's always a sort of a strain to hold back, so that the simplicity can come out, out of the complex. One thread, really. I'm never sure, of course, whether or not I'm doing the right thing. The only thing that's right is what I do. Because what else can you do?

When you say you're never sure whether you're doing the right thing, the fact that you make a sentence and leave it, right up to the publication stage, obviously implies a decision as to its rightness. Well, how do you know it's the right thing?

How does one know? Because you believe you haven't done it? Or that you started wrong and you're still going wrong, but finally you can't alter it? As I say, I need patience, because I still look on myself as a young writer, though God knows I'm not young. I started writing when I was twenty, I got something published when I was thirty, and I'm now in my forties, so I've been writing and publishing for many years, and already seem to have lived a lifetime or two. Two lifetimes, in fact. The idea of writing until I'm seventy-five or eighty — or at sixty, I'll peg out, but anyway, it's still a long time. So patience is not only what one has to have; it's what one can afford to have. If at the moment one is bringing out this simple linear form, one can go on with this: this simple linear form can cover a multitude of complexities. Lots of my stuff already does. As I said in *Raw Material,* I think that a writer tries to write about the complexities of life in as simple a manner as possible, so that a simple person can understand it. This is what one aims for and hopes for. Maybe one just writes about the bloody simplicities in a simple manner and that's that. Everything's so fucking uncertain and yet at the moment, sometimes, one feels particularly confident, even arrogant.

Did you say somewhere that you began Raw Material *with a concept, which was to try and define your origin as a writer, and then proceeded to the practical means of doing it through your grandparents. Is that right, in two steps? Can you say anything about how it hit you or how you found that this was the way of doing it, through your grandparents?*

I'll read you the sentence, from a notebook, that set me off: "Remembering childhood is like looking back on an intense and wonderful love affair that was stamped out by some awful circumstance." The first sentence is from a notebook, but the rest of this short first section just came to me. I wrote the book over seven times.

This is in connection with the need for patience, this tremendous amount of rewriting?

Yes, absolutely, because this little bit here was twenty pages on, then I cut the end out and put it somewhere else, and threw some out, and as I say, I rewrote it seven times.

That is the opening section of the book, but as you've just said, it wasn't written first. Is this a normal pattern for you in the construction of a book? Whereby you construct a whole lot of separate sections and then shuffle them around to find the order of the narrative? Or is that unusual for you?

I've done everything. As you know, one does everything. In *The Death of William Posters*, I wrote a hundred pages or so for the first section and I just condensed it to thirty pages and put it in somewhere else as a flashback, and began somewhere else. All the stuff I took out, I used as a short story, being a miser like all writers.

So you don't throw anything away, you put it by?

I try to. Sometimes they don't work, so you put them by. Some day they may come in useful.

So when you say you've done everything in terms of sequence, you mean you've begun at the beginning and gone to the end, but that you've also begun in the middle. . . .

No, it wouldn't be true to say that . . . but often I've begun and found when it's completed, the first draft, that it would be better to begin thirty pages on because the first thirty pages were getting warmed up or they turned out to be irrelevant, you could put them as two or three pages in the middle of the novel, as somebody's thoughts.

Very often it's your way of coasting into the novel itself?

That's right. On the runway, as it were. If I think back to when I first started writing publishable stories, I go in pretty easily because I know that generally . . . I used to say to people that my first draft was something a child could have written, so sloppy and ungrammatical and loose and weak. Now it's much better, though it still has to be written eight bloody times, no seven, I must be honest, but seven certainly. So I coast in, and the first draft is very bad.

But you're not too distressed by that?

I'm unconcerned.

Are you so delighted the thing is happening at all. . . ?

Maybe.

But what is lacking from your description of the work process is the sweat and agony that a lot of writers make very heavy weather of. Do you omit it because it simply doesn't happen?

The sweat and agony comes when I'm revising. When I've got my first typed copy, then I just go through it and it's torment. I don't want to make too heavy weather of it because what does anybody care? But it's blackened with corrections until I can't read it, with additions and subtractions, so I type it again — clean, marvellous, I think it's a final draft! Then I start reading it, and in about two months' time, it's *black*; type it again, I think, final, terrific, send this off! I start reading it and I think, "Oh, this just doesn't go here at all," and I start shuffling it, and then I've got to type it to see what it reads like, then re-work it under its new arrangement and so on. . . .

That is an editorial, rational, intellectual effort, very hard work — but what about the sort of misery some writers go through when they feel their inspiration's dried up and they'll never write anything good again? Do you go through that? Or is there always a new book, pretty well always a new thing to work on?

First of all, when I'm writing by hand, my first draft, I always feel great — I feel marvellous, I'm sent, I'm writing. That's the best time, then of course you've got to do the work, the spade work. All right, I quite enjoy it, but sometimes I just can't look at it any more, so I have to go chop down trees or whatever.

So you don't suffer from extended periods of nothing? Or desperation that you'll never write another book?

I've always got something pushing on. I'm always editing some stories, or putting a book of poems together, or getting back to a draft of a novel that's no bloody good so I've got to get back to it. And if I didn't write another book in my life, why worry? I've always thought that there's no point in worrying. I expect I will be able to go on writing, somehow. I don't anticipate anything stopping me, but who knows, anything can happen.

And if it did, you'd just take off for a while and let it be?

I was coming to the end of *A Start in Life* and suddenly stopped and couldn't write a word, and I just went back to it eventually. I wasn't worried at all. I was giving it a chance by sitting down and working out what I'd already done, but I wasn't worried, it never occurred to me that I'd never write again.

Do you need to read over stuff to somebody else?

I usually show Ruth what I'm doing, about the second draft. And I like to see what she's writing. We're interested.

Does it go deeper than that? "Interested" is a cool word.

Yes, well, she will say to me, "Getting a bit repetitive there, aren't you?" and I might say, "Well, I am a bit." Or she might say: "This man is over-exaggerated." And I may say: "He's not, don't believe it." And then maybe the next draft I might make him less exaggerated, or I might not.

But essentially you're on your own?

Absolutely, from A to Z I'm on my own. I don't have an editor, I've never allowed an editor to touch anything of mine. I sent *Ragman's Daughter* to *The New Yorker* and they'd pay a lot of money, and an editor there sent back three pages of corrections. He was slowing the story down and altering the punctuation and the colloquial rhythm I'd worked out by reading the story aloud to myself three times. (If ever I'm in doubt or want to perfect something, I read it aloud.) So I sent it back and said: "Very sorry, I've read your corrections carefully and I've considered each one, and if I took them up, it would alter the speed of the story." He wrote back and said: "I see what you mean, but there's still a few," so I got one sheet instead of three. I sent them back again and said, "I can't do it," and he sent them back again and said, "You really ought to, because we are experienced in this." And finally I wrote back and said: "Look, don't try and get rid of your troubles on me. In fact, I don't care; you can keep your money." And they took it. I was amazed. I wasn't being pig-headed, but I really had worked on that story and his corrections would have altered the speed of it. Of course, there's a man at my publisher who says: "Look, you don't spell it that way."

We've tended to refer throughout to your novels. Is your poetry very different for you?

It is, yes. I always thought I was a poet. Between twenty and thirty, even though I was writing novels, I was concentrating just as much on poetry. Poetry is purely inspirational. I don't know how to explain it. I've got nothing to say about it.

Not because there's nothing to say, but because it's so difficult? Because it's even more obscure in its origins than the novels?

The best explanation for all that is probably in Graves's *The White Goddess,* where he explains the whole process of poetic myth and inspiration. Inspiration to him is a white goddess, the great woman myth, but finally I don't go along with it because it's too archaic, too Edwardian, almost as if she were a nanny or a governess, it boils down to that. But finally, you almost wait for poems. You can't wait for a novel, you have to be active. But for poems, you have to be struck or put onto the tracks, as it were.

So when a poem comes, does it begin from a line or an image, or is it the whole thing received?

It begins with an image, and sometimes it's complete. Sometimes I've written a complete poem straight down, in a similar situation to writing the *Long-Distance Runner* story, like a lightning flash, but it's quicker. The poems I write down complete obviously tend to be short poems. If you write it out ten or twelve times before it's finalized, as I do, then of course you tend to lengthen it. Or not, sometimes not if you value it, it depends.

Is it the more successful ones that are received complete?

I think so. An example is *The Poem Left by a Dead.* There are others.

When a particular image or thought comes to you, are you ever uncertain whether it's poem or prose?

I'm never uncertain about that. I don't know why. That's me, of course; reviewers have often said it's difficult to tell.

One last thing. Do you see a progression in your work from "early" to "middle", and do you look forward to "late"? Or does this not concern you?

It's a matter of timing. Time is so long, one hopes. When you produce a book, reviewers say: "Where's he going now?" There's a progression, but not in that sense, one is not "going any-where." One is an entity which, hopefully, will continually expand and enrich. To get back to what I said — the best writing you can do is to produce the complexities in a simple manner. This may be impossible to do because if it comes out in a simple way it can't be complex. I don't know; this is what we have to find out. I don't think it has to be impossible or contradictory. If you've got something to say, say it as plainly as possible, and as time goes on, this will become more possible.

So, the question was about progression, or development of style: are you suggesting that your development is or ideally should be toward greater simplicity?

I would say so, but how it's going to turn out in practice I don't know. . . .

How is it turning out? Looking back, can you detect any development, or is this just critics' games?

No, well, it might be a bit early . . . but I can see expansion, you know? I'm more competent, and more confident. I am able to deal with situations and different zones, which I feel were not so open to me fifteen years ago. Most parts of *A Tree On Fire* I couldn't have written when I was twenty-five. And the speed with which I carried through *A Start in Life,* and bringing in so much, I couldn't have brought it in then because I just didn't have the experience, either of writing or of life.

Yes, but that is development not towards simplicity but towards an ever richer mixture, isn't it?

Yes, but that can be produced in a simple way too. Stylistic-ally, one is simple, but the experience you're reproducing on paper isn't necessarily simple. Again, put complicated experiences on paper but keep your style simple. It's not really saying much, finally.

You seem able to trust your natural rhythms. That's a great luxury for a writer, to be able to give his own instincts time to work themselves out.

I'm dead lucky, it's true.

One of the most astonishing things, personally, I found about what you've said was about your attitude to time. It contrasts strongly with my own. You view your life as a long life, whereas I think of life as so short that I have a sort of desperate anxiety about how to spend the next three hours, with the result that I spend it less well. . . . It's not just a matter of economics, but of temperament. You don't have that urgency?

I have this feeling that beyond me, which I can't reach, is another rhythm. What I mean is this: I've written over a dozen books, and I have a feeling which says that if I'd been more patient, more of an artist, instead of those twelve, I might have written three books, and really taken my time, and really held myself back, slowly, to bring it out, my natural rhythm, you see [*laughs*], instead of racing through so many books. It's only a feeling, there's nothing one can do about it. Finally I think, "Fuck it, Stendhal wrote *Charterhouse of Parma* in six weeks." I'm not making any comparisons except that we all feel there's something we're not doing right. I seem to be bone idle, I don't seem to do much work, I seem to be out there in my garden digging, cutting vegetation down. I seem to peg along, you know, I go away for a week, or up to Nottingham for a time, and at the end of it, I've got a book out, you see. I'm not aware of working away, but if I wrote the book out seven times in fourteen months, I must have worked. I love to work at night, yeah, nine at night till one in the morning, that's great.

You don't like to look out there, through the windows on to your garden, while you work?

After a while, it's just like a picture hung on the wall, it's never-changing, you know.

Never changing? [Laughs]

Not much. It gets a bit barren in the winter.

Alan Burns

Alan Burns was born in London, where he was called to the Bar (Middle Temple) in 1956 and after post-graduate research in politics at the London School of Economics worked as a libel lawyer for Beaverbrook Newspapers. He began writing full-time in 1961 and has published seven novels — *Buster* (1961), *Europe After the Rain* (1965), *Celebrations* (1967), *Babel* (1969), *Dreamerika!* (1972), *The Angry Brigade* (1975), *The Day Daddy Died* (1981) — and a book on censorship, *To Deprave and Corrupt* (1972). His play *Palach* (1970) was produced by Charles Marowitz at the Open Space Theatre, London, and published in 1974. In 1969 and 1973 Burns received Writing Bursaries from the Arts Council of Great Britain. He was Henfield Writing Fellow at the School of English & American Studies, University of East Anglia, in 1971, and in 1973 became C. Day Lewis Writing Fellow in London. During 1975 he was writer-in-residence at the Western Australian Institute of Technology, and in 1976 held the Arts Council Writing Fellowship at the City Literary Institute, London. He is now Associate Professor of English at the University of Minnesota.

In the following conversation Charles Sugnet asks Alan Burns (who has been called by Angus Wilson "one of the two or three most interesting new novelists working in England") many of the same questions Burns himself put to other writers in this volume.

SUGNET: *Alan, you were educated as a barrister and practised law for some years, how did you begin to write?*
BURNS: The answer is "with difficulty" and over a period of time. The prerequisite for shifting from the law to writing is to be a bad lawyer, and I managed that quite successfully. I had been trying to write for years, since I was a kid. I had a hankering for it but couldn't get it right. But I can pinpoint the breakthrough precisely. I was walking down Fleet Street and noticed a jeweller's window. There was a silver frame for sale and in the frame a photograph of a youngish couple kissing, embracing. It was a sweet photo, rather old-fashioned, probably from the 'thirties, and it rang a bell because I'd seen a similar photo in the family album, of my father and mother kissing on their honeymoon in Monte Carlo, with orange trees in the background. I had long wanted to write about my parents and the love between

them and the not-love between them but I didn't know where to start. At that moment I realized I needn't tackle their psychology or their histories, I could start with a picture. I discovered the power of the image. A day or two later I got out the family album and spent a weekend with it, looking and describing and thinking about that photo. And that became a starting point for my first book, *Buster*. Needless to say, the fruits of that weekend were reduced to a line and a half, but I had got going. From then on I found I could do the same with other episodes of the early life which was the subject of that novel. I would shut my eyes, sort of "take snaps" of the past and describe them one by one, until I had a sequence.

Is that how a book begins for you, with an image?

It never again began that way. It began more obliquely, not with pictures but words — a phrase I stumbled on that made an impression.

Do you have a title to guide you before the book takes shape?

Sometimes. The title is important. Difficulty over selecting a title usually means something's wrong. If I can't get the title right probably I can't say what the book is about; maybe it's too diffuse and needs pulling together. I stole my best title, *Europe After the Rain*, from that marvellous painting by Max Ernst.

What else do you work with? Do you use index cards?

Well, the high technology . . . consists of a pair of scissors, paste and, most important, a large table top so I can place things side by side. I don't like leafing through card indexes though I should use one because I often lose things. I can spend a day looking for a phrase, after it's been cut up and reduced to a tiny sliver of paper; I'll be on my knees looking for it, because I use the floor when I run out of table space. I start from chaos and work towards order. I accumulate as large a mass of raw material as possible and then try to order it. But you can have too much material. It can be an ocean you drown or flounder in, and find so many patterns, so many connections that the book, which must be contained between hard covers, eludes you. That was my experience with my latest novel. I spent five years amassing material, being prevented largely by circumstances from writing the book. When I eventually started at page one, I was flummoxed. For a week or two I didn't know where to start.

When you talk of organizing your work you mention photographs, table tops — what you're describing is spatial rather than temporal. It doesn't consist of putting material in time sequence, the way some novelists might do. You're talking of the kind of inspiration that comes by juxtaposing things in space?

Sequence in time is unavoidable, given the linear nature of the novel; "that happened, then that happened, then that happened," is very important to me, but the more obscure those connections, the clearer I have to be in the decisions I take as to what comes next.

In your books in the late 'sixties and early 'seventies, Europe After the Rain, Babel *and* Celebrations, *the texture is clearly avant-garde and somewhat difficult of access. But in* The Angry Brigade *you moved away from that towards a surface that appears simpler.*

You say I moved away, I have more of a sense that I was moved away. First, I think I was at a dead end. Particularly in *Babel,* but also in *Dreamerika!,* I had fragmented myself out of existence and, this side of sanity, I don't think I could have done any more with that. I had to do something else. Secondly, I had driven myself into a certain corner in relation to the readers who were interested enough in my work to buy the books. There were not enough of them! That's the negative aspect, the place I was pushed out of. As to where I went, I was influenced by a speech made by Heinrich Böll on receiving the Nobel Prize for Literature. He took a strong political line, saying there was no point in writing for the few, one had to find a language that was accessible, close to "the language of the people". In *The Angry Brigade* I tried to do something of the kind.

The book appears to consist of interviews and conversations, but it's more complicated than that?

Yes. The Angry Brigade was the name of an anarchist group that made an impact on London some years ago. . . . No one could be sure who the members were. I purported to have discovered them and the book contained what seemed to be a series of tape-recorded interviews with them. Needless to say it was fiction and those "interviews" were mainly conducted with my friends on topics quite other than those discussed by the characters in the book. To give a rather curious example: I had a friend, a young woman, who had to visit the dentist on a number of occasions. This dismal experience was made worse by the fact that as she sat there the dentist and his nurse, between whom there seemed to be something cooking, would gossip away one to the other, excluding the patient, apart from giving her mouth an occasional prod with a chromium instrument. My friend described this in rather threatened and unhappy tones. A radically rewritten version of my friend's story is used in the novel: there's a character on the periphery of the Brigade itself who describes going to one of their meetings, sitting in a chair being aware there were things going on that she was not part of, being distressed and disturbed and a bit frightened. That's typical of hundreds of similar transformations I attempted in that book.

So you were able to make a book that was accessible on its surface yet complex enough to be satisfying to write. As to your latest novel, The Day Daddy Died, *what is its style?*

In so far as I have those two different styles available to me, and my tendency is to alternate between them, this is the book maybe in which those styles meet. The book is composed of a number of strands. The first I call the "Norah" strand. It revolves round a woman I knew some years ago in London, a remarkable woman, about fifty when I knew her, blonde hair, wonderful skin, blue eyes, a working-class woman, very tough indeed, married once, five children by five fathers. I spent hours talking with her. Hers seemed to me an extraordinary and exemplary life. However, as often happens, when I came to review the material it was nowhere near interesting enough. It was a great story, yet the quality of spoken language on its own wasn't enough.

A year or so later I began a short story of about twenty pages. I suppose I was bouncing back from the conversational style for I wrote it in high-powered language, with complex juxtapositions of images and all the rest. It was the story of a series of sexual encounters between an older man and a young girl. When I finished it I was dissatisfied; it seemed mannered, a bit self-indulgent, and sexy in the wrong way. So I put that to one side. During the years 1974–7 I travelled a good deal, from Britain to Australia and back, then to the United States. I gathered a load of disparate material on the way, including "found" letters and various other stuff. I had boxes full of material. . . . The break-through came when I saw how these different stories fitted together. Norah, whose father died when she was twelve, lived the rest of her life ricocheting from man to man, bearing a child by each. Of course the men in her life were successive manifestations of the father she's searching for, without making too heavy psychological weather of it; and the second story was about an older man and a younger girl. I could marry those two strands.

One question you often asked other writers was how their unconscious life bears on their work. You asked about their dreams and whether they were able to tap their instinct or their unconscious. Do you have any techniques that you are aware of for doing this or do you let it happen in the dark, taking its own course?

Maybe it is best described as "letting it happen in the dark", although if that indicates that I make active use of dreams as such, I don't. . . . However I've found various ways through to that territory. One is a technique I could call the "eyes blur". When I was writing *Europe After the Rain* I was very unsure about the setting. I knew it had to be a foreign place but I didn't know where. In a second-hand bookshop in Lyme Regis I came across a book by an English reporter who'd been to Poland and written a strong, straightforward journalist's description of post-war life there in about 1946. I knew that it could provide the key to the background. What I did was, I put the book by the side of my typewriter. Then I "looked" at the page. I looked yet didn't look. I did that thing painters often do, which is to screw up their eyes so only bits and pieces percolate through. I typed, forgetting what I was about, that I was writing a novel, blocking out . . . as much of the rational mind as I could. I picked out images, not always the most startling, not worrying about connections, just batting away for a week or two. Of course the result derived partly from a conscious decision: I spotted the book and saw how to use it. . . . And of course the raw material was transformed, re-worked through a number of drafts. I also use Burroughs's cut-up technique which I insist I invented because I used it before I'd heard of Burroughs. . . . I create a sea of images and disconnected phrases in which I find the stories.

Again the techniques you're describing are spatial, the analogy with painting and so on; and your new novel has photographs in it as well as your text?

They are a series of collages by Ian Breakwell who's been film-making, painting, writing, performing, for some years. He's a successful professional artist, a very good one, and a friend of mine for years. Ian refuses, quite properly, to call them illustrations. The collages don't give another version of what is already in the text; it isn't Little Nell in an etching. He has constructed a narrative that runs parallel. I don't know if his work acts as an undercurrent or an overcurrent, because pictures make such a tremendous impact, words have some difficulty in standing up to them. I wanted to describe the adult life of a girl whose father died when she was twelve and follow her right through till she was fifty. I needed to keep the living memory of that father-relationship going through the book. I used recollection and recurrent image as a way of keeping that strand going, but it's wonderful to have another self-sufficient narrative to reinforce that. . . .

How did you and Breakwell work together?

On the 'phone I told him something about the book and he was interested, enough for me to say, Okay, I'll send you . . . now what I had to send him at that stage was a fairly early draft, fifty or sixty pages. He considered them for quite a while and then did a series of rough pictures and sent me a Xerox of them. By that time I was further into the text. . . . It worked beautifully, we were both pleased with it.

So the early text triggered the first photos, and the later text was influenced by the early photos?

Precisely.

How do history and politics press in on your work?

It changes constantly. Early in writing I was naive enough to think I could change the world, a little. Or even quite a lot. That was the prime purpose of my writing. . . . I still feel it is impossible to understand the world without looking at it to some extent through marxist spectacles. Apart from national movements and the big tides of history, you cannot have enough understanding of the relationship between people, not only between boss and worker but between father and son, women and men, without that analysis of class relationships and the nature of capitalism and its decay into imperialism. . . . But I can't call myself a Marxist because I don't live, work or fight that way. Nor do I label myself Freudian, Jungian, Kropotkinite . . . though I've been influenced by those ideas and by countless others.

What about the relationship between the writer and the reader? To what extent is it a political decision to simplify your style?

There's a bit of that in it. There's a lot else too. There's also my reaction to being clobbered by certain critics on the grounds of obscurity and my initial resentment against their attacks, giving way to a long-term self-analysis, and a feeling that I need a wider audience. Also, there was a time when I was really intent on and by the skin of my teeth managing to live by writing, so I absolutely had to have a larger audience. . . .

Every aspect of the writing process — the selection of type-writer and the kind of paper and the conditions of the room and the collection of material and the proof-reading and okaying the book jacket — every step in that operation is great; I love it all. The only aspect of writing that is not good is the economics. . . . No payment for a book came anywhere near keeping me during the time it took to write it, because I write very slowly.

It's unusual for you to write a short story — why is that?

John Gardner calls this being a "big breath" writer. It's a nice phrase. I think there's a sort of rightness-and-tightness, precious-ness, about a short, a little thing. I find even in the best short stories a neatness and inescapable artificiality as opposed to the novel "heavy with life". Angus Wilson says something along these lines. . . . I like the piece of work that I embark on to make — at least to attempt — a big bound.

You've done a couple of short things, though, one a piece called "Wonderland" — how did that come about?

I was asked for it and found myself able to do it. But *The Day Daddy Died* grew out of "Wonderland"; so the short piece was the precursor of a novel. To me the novel is the grand art form of this century: it is so vital, so flexible, so eloquent, so compendious. If I want to have that sense of adventure, I need that big area, I need the wonderfully open generous form that the novel is, which allows me ample space in which to explore.

Index of names

169